STANLEY HAYAMI, NISEI SON

His Diary, Letters, and Story
From an American Concentration Camp to Battlefield
1942–1945

Annotated by Joanne Oppenheim

Foreword by Senator Daniel Inouye

Brick Tower, New York

To Stanley Kunio Hayami.

Let his dreams for a better future inspire you to use your talents, treasure your freedom, and defend the civil liberties he should never have lost!

Brick Tower Press
1230 Park Avenue
New York, New York 10128

© Joanne Oppenheim, 2008

Library of Congress Cataloging-in-Publication Data
Oppenheim, Joanne.

Stanley Hayami, Nisei Son / Joanne Oppenheim.—1st ed.

p. cm.

Includes bibliographical references.
1. Japanese Americans—Evacuation and relocation, 1942–1945—Juvenile literature. 2. Hayami, Stanley. 1925–1945—Juvenile literature. 3. World War, 1939–1945—Japanese American literature. 4.World War, 1939–1945-Personal Narratives, American—Juvenile literature. 5. World War 1939–1945—Participation, Japanese Americans—Juvenile literature. 6. World War 1939–1945—Japanese Americans—Prisoners of Conscience—Juvenile literature. 7. World War, 1939–1945—442nd Regimental Combat Team—United States—Juvenile literature. I. Title.

ISBN 10: 1-883283-67-1
ISBN 13: 978-1-883283-67-4.

Library of Congress Control Number: 2008934008
First Edition, November 2008

Cover design by James Oppenheim
Book design by Joan Auclair

CONTENTS

FOREWORD

On a recent visit to the Japanese American National Museum in Los Angeles, I saw a photograph of Pvt. Stanley Hayami, a young soldier I remember from so many years ago. It was his warm smile that made him so instantly recognizable. Although Stanley Hayami was from the mainland and I was from Hawaii, we both served in the 2nd Battalion, Company "E" of the 442nd Regimental Combat Team. Both of us fought in the Italian campaign to break through the Gothic Line, Germany's last line of defense. In late April of 1945, we were both in the battle to take the town of San Terenzo, during the final days of World War II in Europe.

All of us in the 442nd, the all-Nisei combat team, were not always friends. Those of us from Hawaii didn't trust the mainland boys who spoke correct English like the plantation bosses on the islands. They seemed arrogant, they snickered at the way we talked (Pidgin English) and called us "buddaheads." We had a name for them, too. Our disagreements were often settled with fists, and we dubbed the mainland boys "kotunks," for that was the sound their heads made when they hit the ground.

The animosity continued to grow until we received an invitation to visit places called Rohwer and Jerome in Arkansas. We thought the Army was sending us to towns where Japanese Americans lived. But to our horror, we found ourselves in a so-called relocation camp where the inmates looked like us! Not until we were escorted into the compound by armed men in American uniforms did we realize that the mainland boys and their families had been incarcerated. In Hawaii, the vast majority of those of Japanese descent were not imprisoned. I remember wondering at that time what I would have done if my family were inside of such a place. And to this day, I ask myself the question: would I have volunteered to serve if I had been in that camp? Our visits to Arkansas changed everything.

After that, the Nisei of Hawaii and the mainland became brothers. We were truly a united force and we all fought knowing that we were not just fighting for our country but the ugly prejudice that our families and friends had faced because we looked like the enemy.

We were all so young and full of hope. Stanley did not live to make his youthful dreams come true. But his diary lives on as a reminder that what happened then must never happen again . . . and that we must defend our liberties (and those of others) at home as well as abroad.

Senator Daniel Inouye
Washington, D.C.

*STANLEY HAYAMI: Mark Keppel Hi,
San Gabriel, Calif.; "Tempo," Art Ed.;
"Has a way with pen and ink."*

*Stanley's senior year photo and entry in Tempo, the Heart
Mountain High School annual of the Class of 1944.*

INTRODUCTION

Several years ago, while researching a book about Japanese Americans during World War II, I found the story of Stanley Hayami. He was a 16-year-old boy who began keeping a diary in November 1942, when he was a prisoner of his own country, although he had committed no crime. Stanley was an American citizen of Japanese ancestry who found his life turned upside down when war began between the United States and Japan.

Stan's diary serves as witness to a dark time in our history and is told through the eyes of a teenager who will soon be expected to take up the responsibility of a man. As you read his diary, you will discover Stan's creative talents, as well as his idealism, his optimism, and his aspirations. He has a quirky sense of humor, along with a more serious side, and dreams of a "United Nations of Earth." He talks to his diary as a confidant, a safe place to express his opinions and record the everyday events of his life. No one told him he had to keep a journal. He wrote because he needed a private place to keep his ideas and think through the contradictions of his life.

In many ways, Stan seems like a typical high school student. He had grown up going to American schools, watching American sports, speaking American slang, singing American songs, eating American food. Yet Stan was anything but a typical American. During the summer of 1942, Stanley Hayami lived in a horse stall with his parents, his sister, Grace, and two brothers, Frank and Walter.

The Hayamis, like all people of Japanese ancestry who lived on the West Coast, were no longer free. Naoichi Hayami, Stanley's father, had been in America for thirty-five years when the war began. He arrived in San Francisco on April 13, 1906, aboard the *S.S. Mongolia,* just days before the great earthquake and fire that almost destroyed the city. Luckily, 18-year-old Naoichi left for San Jose before the disaster struck.

For the next twelve years Naoichi worked hard at a variety of jobs, saving enough

Naoichi Hayami was a teenager when he arrived in San Francisco aboard the S.S.Mongolia.

Young Japanese women arriving at Angel Island in California. Many were "picture brides"— their marriages arranged by exchanging photos.

money finally to send for a bride. Asano Osafune was only a little girl of eight when Naoichi left Japan. They were neighbors in Hiroshima, where they both grew up. Asano was twenty when she arrived in San Pedro, California aboard the S.S. Anyo Maru on November 5, 1918. Together, she and Naoichi worked long hard hours to make a better life in America for themselves and their children.

They were Issei, members of the first generation of Japanese who immigrated to the United States. They were prohibited by racist laws that prevented all Asians from becoming naturalized citizens of the United States. The Issei were "involuntary aliens" while their children, the Nisei, the second generation, were American citizens by birth.

With the start of World War II, the Issei, who were officially legal aliens, suddenly became "enemy aliens" and the Nisei became "non-aliens"—a label intended to chip away at their legal status as citizens. Politicians and white supremacists used the war as an opportunity to accomplish their long-standing goal of getting rid of the Nikkei, all those of Japanese descent, and seizing the farmland they had turned into fertile fields.

Instead of defending the Nikkei, the government gave in to lies and rumors that the Nikkei were loyal to the Emperor of Japan and could not be trusted. Editorials of racist journalists and politicians represented the interests of groups such as the Sons and Daughters of the Golden West, the Grange, American Legion, and others who wanted to keep America white. The Nikkei were not charged with or tried for any crime. Yet, they were easy to target as suspects who might blow up bridges, poison the water supply, or send signals to the Japanese. In fact, not one of them was ever found guilty of any unpatriotic act. Not one Japanese American was ever found guilty of sabotage or spying.

The "whole mess," as Stan put it, began on December 7, 1941, when the Japanese government attacked the United States, sinking most of the United States Pacific fleet in Hawaii. On the following day the United States declared war on Japan and for those of Japanese descent, life would never be the same.

On December 7th and for weeks afterwards, the FBI arrested hundreds of the Issei leaders of the Nikkei community. They were immigrants; most had come to the United States 30 to 40 years earlier. Some were fishermen who were suspected of being spies who would send messages to the enemy. They were merchants, journalists, and others with business connections in Japan. Some were leaders of Japanese American churches and Japanese language schools. Those who had simply traveled back to visit relatives in Japan were on the list of suspects and taken away to prisons run by the Dept. of Justice. Some eventually returned to their families. Others were interned for the duration. Not one of the people arrested was ever charged, tried or found guilty of any crime. But they were held on suspicion and separated from their families for as many as four years.

At first, it seemed that only the Issei would be imprisoned. Yet, in just a matter of months, fear and rumors were spread as false alarms of enemy air raids set off sirens in the night and newspapers and politicians pressured Washington to imprison the Nikkei. On February 19, 1942 President Franklin Delano Roosevelt signed Executive Order 9066, and although Japanese Americans were not mentioned in the document, it opened the door that led to the largest mass imprisonment in American history. That order gave the Army the right to declare a "military zone" up and down the West Coast and empowered them remove anyone they chose from those areas.

In signing that order President Roosevelt turned the fate of 120,000 men, women, and children of Japanese descent into the hands of Lt Gen. John DeWitt, the commander of the West Coast Defense Command. DeWitt made no distinction between the enemy Japanese and Japanese Americans. In a memo to the Secretary of War he wrote, "the Japanese race is an enemy race and while many second and third generation Japanese born on U.S. soil, possessed of United States citizenship, have become 'Americanized' the racial strains are undiluted."

By late spring 1942, Western portions of California, Washington, Oregon and

WORDS TO KNOW

Issei	First generation of Japanese who immigrated to the USA.
Nisei	Second generation, children of the Issei, born in America, they were citizens.
Kibei	Second generation, born in America, like the Nisei, but educated in Japan.
Sansei	Third generation Japanese Americans, children of Nisei and Kibei.
Yonsei	Fourth generation Japanese Americans.
Nikkei	Name for all people of Japanese ancestry in America.
Ojisan	Uncle.
Obasan	Aunt.

Arizona were declared as military zones that the Nikkei community was forced to leave. They were imprisoned temporarily in so-called assembly centers until more permanent prisons could be built. Most had less than a week to try to sell, store, or abandon their possessions. They were allowed to bring only what they could carry and as they left they had no way of knowing where they would be taken.

Stan and his family were swept up in the largest mass roundup in our country's history. On May 14, 1942 the Hayamis, along with thousands of others, were taken to the Pomona Fairgrounds, one of 16 Assembly Centers where the Nikkei were temporarily imprisoned until more permanent Relocation Centers were built. The government chose racetracks and fair grounds, because they offered ready-made "housing" in the form of horse stalls and barns that reeked of their former tenants.

In the late summer of '42, the Nikkei were forced to make a second evacuation. They were moved further inland, to one of the ten War Relocation Authority's (WRA) Camps that had been hastily built in isolated places far from their homes on the West Coast. Thousands were sent to the brutal heat of the Arizona desert, to Native American reservation land, others to Colorado, Utah, Arkansas, Idaho, and Wyoming. The Hayamis were moved from Pomona to Heart Mountain in Wyoming.

Before the war ended more than 120,000 people of Japanese descent would be forced to leave their homes, jobs, schools, friends, and the lives they had known. Despite the fact that he was born in the United States and a citizen, Stan was to spend the next two and a half years of his life imprisoned by his own government, behind barbed wire fences, guarded by armed military police.

In November of 1942, Stan Hayami began keeping a diary that captures the harsh reality of Wyoming and his personal struggles as a student, son, brother, friend, and citizen of the world, who despite all obstacles, holds onto his dreams of the future. It is his optimism that continues to shine through his diary, and his determination to improve himself as well as the world. His dreams will inspire those who work to build a world where differences are not met with racism and war, but with respect for others and kindness that allows all people to live in harmony and with dignity.

Painting by Stanley Hayami from his dairy.

Our city really looks like something at night. Row on row of lights and from a distance it looks like a real city. It gives one a sort of queer feeling tho to look out over the area at night with all the lights on and then realize that the city houses a race of people who because of their race have been isolated from society under very trying and difficult conditions, and many of whom may never return to their original homes and property. War is a cruel thing. Seems that man with his brilliant mind could find a humane substitute for war. Am afraid tho that as long as there are nations there will be war.

Diary of John A. Nelson, Administrative Officer, Heart Mountain

11

Asano Hayami

Naoichi Hayami

Frank

Stan

Sach (Grace)

Walt

MEET THE HAYAMI FAMILY

Before you begin Stanley Hayami's diary, meet Frank Hayami, his older brother, whose letter will introduce you to their family. Frank wrote this brief family history in 1992, many years after the events recorded in Stan's diary. Frank's letter was written to Mike Mackey, who was then a graduate student, writing a thesis on Heart Mountain. In 1942, Frank had just graduated from Berkeley and was on the threshold of beginning his career when the incarceration put his life on hold. Perhaps it was generational or because this was written long after the events, but Frank's sense of injustice and anger are apparent and less reserved than Stanley's. His straightforward words will transport you to that time and place . . .

My full name is Frank Yutaka Hayami and I was the oldest of four children. My father gave us all an American name because he wanted us to grow up as full-fledged American citizens. Then he gave us a Japanese middle name because he feared that he might be forced to return to Japan with his family because of the anti-Japanese feelings in those days in California and the fact that Japanese nationals were not eligible for American citizenship, nor were they permitted to purchase land or enjoy the other benefits of full American life.

Of course, later on my parents were permitted to send their American sons into battle for the cause of liberty while they were being detained in the camp, denied the right to return to their home in California and denied the right to US citizenship afforded to all European nationals . . . sorry . . . I didn't mean to get on the soap-box.

My family and I lived in San Gabriel, California, a small suburban town located about 10 miles east of LA. We had lived there since 1931. My father ran a small, mom-and-pop nursery with all of us kids helping out . . . there were six in the family: Mom (43), Pop (53), and four kids, Walt (13), Stan (16), Grace (19) [and myself] Frank.

I was about 22 . . . in my fifth year at the Univ. of California in Berkeley majoring in Electrical Engineering when a foreign country, Japan, attacked my country, the United States, at Pearl Harbor and forever changed my life as it did to millions of others. Since I had enough credits, my diploma was mailed to me and I graduated college with a Bachelor's degree in Engineering when the mailman threw the diploma onto my cot at camp.

I was detained at the Pomona Fairgrounds Horse Stalls and Heart Mountain . . . When I first saw Heart Mountain, my heart sank. Bleak, scrubby, dusty, barren, desolate. Not a tree in sight. Dust stirring in the breeze. And row on row of those somber tar-papered shacks that were to be our shelter for the duration, all surrounded by barbed wire fencing and guard towers standing tall at each corner with armed American soldiers, guarding American citizens.

Frank Hayami to Mike Mackey, Oct. 16, 1992

Soon after the Hayamis arrived at Heart Mountain the winter snows began. It was no ordinary winter. Temperatures dipped to 28 degrees below. Old-timers acknowledged it was one of the harshest winters on record in Wyoming. For southern Californians without proper clothing, living in barracks with no insulation, life was extremely harsh. Add to this, a growing resentment that the government would treat them and their American-born children as if they were enemy prisoners.

His country had been at war for almost a year when Stan started his diary . . .

Diary of Stanley Hayami

1942–1944

NOTE:

Stanley's diary is reproduced as he wrote it. There are gaps in time because he did not write an entry each day. Along with his diary are letters and interviews of friends and family that enlarge the story told through his diary and letters. His dairy is in chronological order, so if you prefer to read just the diary, you can skip over the narrative portions of the text. The narrative is designed to give the reader more background into the events than the diary alone provides. This is not intended as a history of the incarceration, but rather as a view of that time.

Stan and other people repeatedly use the word "Jap" throughout the text. This word is regarded as an unacceptable, offensive ethnic slur today. We leave it as written because it reflects the climate of that time in history.

His misspellings or grammatical errors were not corrected in order to allow Stan to speak in his own voice. These were the private thoughts of an ordinary teenager, not a memoir written for publication.

All the drawings, unless otherwise noted, are by Stanley Hayami. Most are from the diary, some were for *Tempo,* the 1944 school annual, and some were from Stan's letters. The small cartoons are from *Tempo* and are unsigned. We believe Stanley did these as well.

1942

November 29, 1942

Today I am writing my first entry in this journal. It is no special day, but I have to start someplace.

Right now Walt is listening to Gene Krupa so I don't feel much like writing. Sack is talking with Ma & Pa about leaving camp and going to college & if so what school.

Today I went to sunday school and then saw a football game. It was really cold out there watching that game — there was snow on the ground & it was snowing slightly.

Well I'll be darned they've finally decided to let Sack go to college; its to be Washington U. In St. Louis. Mo. She's majoring in dress design.

Frank isn't home right now like he always isn't. He's probably playing for the dance tonite. I don't understand Frank very well, in his few stops at our house (I mean room) which he's supposed to be living in, he managed to get mad at me sometime last week & I guess he's still mad.

Well thats about all for now I guess. Gotta get up early tomorrow & get braced for the great bad news — Report cards.

1942

November 29, 1942

Today I am writing my first entry in this journal. It is no special day, but I have to start someplace.

Right now Walt is listening to Gene Krupa. I don't feel much like writing. Sach is talking with Ma & Pa about leaving camp and going to college and if so what school.

Today I went to Sunday school and then I saw a football game. It was really cold out there watching that game—there was snow on the ground and it was snowing slightly.

Well I'll be darned they've finally decided to let Sach go to college; it's to be Washington U. in St. Louis, Mo. She's majoring in dress design.

Frank isn't home right now—like he always isn't. He's probably playing for the dance tonight. I don't understand Frank very well, in his few stops at our house (I mean room) which he's supposed to be living in, he managed to get mad at me sometime last week and I guess he's still mad.

Well that's about all for now I guess. Gotta get up early tomorrow and get braced for the great bad news—report cards.

It had to be hard studying in a dimly lit barrack while his kid brother is listening to the radio blaring with the most famous drummer of the day, Gene Krupa. Between Walt's big band music and his parents debating with his older sister, Sachiko, who wants to go off to college, it's a wonder Stan got any work done. Sachiko's American name was Grace, but Stan usually calls her "Sach," her Japanese nickname.

Allowing a daughter to go out into the world was a tough decision for their parents' generation. She was young to be on her own, especially in a world that had turned on them. There was no way of knowing when they would see her once they agreed to let her go. Yet, in Heart Mountain, Sach's life was on hold. Unless they allowed her to leave, she would have to work at some meaningless job. Sach was pleading for a better choice. Soon after the war began the Quaker American Friends Service Committee created the National Japanese American Student Relocation Council that helped more than 4,000 college age students leave the camps and enter more than 600 colleges. Now, Sach would be one of them and Stan hoped to do the same when he graduated in two more years.

In just a few months, their tightly knit family changed radically. Frank was never at home, and home is now a crowded, noisy, single room. The entire family rarely ate together anymore. Frank was well aware of his parents' losses and the changes they were forced to accept. Frank's letter continues . . .

> I realize the great trauma that my parents went through. Forced to leave their comfortable home and nursery business, limited to $100 a month bank withdrawal, loss of their lifetime of hard work, denied the right of American citizenship, humiliated by being treated as common criminals and jailed without the right to a fair trial, herded in to a concentration camp and forced to live in cramped quarters, it is a wonder they retained their sanity. I realize now that it was a time of great despair for them . . . family life disintegrated . . . the younger people would eat with their friends and their siblings and not with their parents. This led to a breakdown in family values. I would return to my bed only at night not having seen my parents for the entire day.
>
> *Frank Hayami letter to Mike Mackey, Oct. 16, 1992*

Nov 30 Mon.
> *Well today I got my report card. Wasn't as bad as I thought*
>
> | | | |
> |---|---|---|
> | *English A* | *Advanced Alg. A* | *Spanish B* |
> | *History A* | *Chemistry B* | |
>
> *Compared to the grades I used to get back home this is lousy. Back home I got straight A's. But considering the competition at this school its not bad. I'm going to try as hard as I can next semester to try to see if I can't raise my Spanish and Chemistry grades up to an A, too. I thought I should have got an A in Spanish, but no use arguing with the teacher he's probably right. My grades next semester will have to be good enough to have no doubts.*
>
> *Today the first copy of our Times subscription came. It makes me feel as if I were at home again.*

Throughout the diary there are echoes of longing for home. Home, although it had its own problems, was often in their thoughts. Walt Hayami recalled his old school in San Gabriel . . .

There were about 30 kids in my class and I was the only Japanese. It was the same in Stan's class. Maybe there were 5 or 6 Japanese in the whole school; the rest were Hispanic and Caucasian. There was a little bit of prejudice—little things like I wouldn't be invited to birthday parties—things like that. Social functions—but I was too young for it to register much.

Walter Hayami interview with author, Nov. 4, 2004

Walt said that he was not as serious about school as his older brothers or sister. He jokingly calls himself the "black sheep," but he remembers Stan found school in Heart Mountain a lot harder than his school in San Gabriel.

School during that first year was especially challenging. Not only were they attending classes in barracks with no desks, there was a shortage of books, science equipment, and basic needs such as adequate heat and bathrooms. Walls between classrooms did not go to the ceilings, so the sounds from adjoining classrooms were a constant distraction. Sheets of plasterboard were black on one side, so they were nailed up and used as blackboards. Students shared the latrines that were also used by more than 300 people in that neighboring block. Yet, for Stan the physical discomforts were not the greatest challenge. School had always come easy to him. In Heart Mountain he had a different worry as his brother, Walt recalls . . .

Stan was an excellent student before the war. It was very easy for him to achieve A's. He could turn the class curve . . .the competition was much less. But when he got into Heart Mountain, he had all these over achieving students that he had to compete with. They were quite smart, but Stan was always up for a challenge.

Walter Hayami interview with author, Nov. 4, 2004

For Stan the competition grew into a continuing struggle throughout his high school years. Some students would have given up, but Stan was persistent. Nor did he give up his interest in the world outside. While many people say they felt cut off from the war and did not follow the latest events, Stan read the newspaper, listened to the radio, and kept himself informed about the world news beyond the confines of Heart Mountain.

Dec. 1, 1942 Tues.

The crunch of snow underfoot . . . the barracks with snow covering them with white. I never saw it or touched it until I came here.

Today I read in the paper that the French Fleet blew itself up. Almost all were sunk by the French themselves so Germany wouldn't take them and use them against the Allies. It happened at Toulon about Friday I guess, because our paper is about four days late. There were about 60 ships in all I guess stuff like that eventually go down in history books.

Stan followed the war news and brought it to life.

It was true that the French sank their fleet so the Germans could not use them; they did not blow the ships up with bombs, however. They scuttled them, flooding them with water until they sank. Stan's drawings of these events are the kinds of typical drawings boys made in and out of the camps.

In fact, one of the teachers in the lower grades was annoyed with a little boy in her class who repeatedly drew pictures of airplanes covered with Japanese flags. One day the teacher finally walked to the boy's desk, picked up his tablet, tore out his airplane pictures, ripped the sheets into small scraps, and told the boy, "We will have no more pictures of any flag but the American flag."

Of course, the boy drawing those planes may have been replaying the events of December 7th. But that is not how his teacher saw it. Patriotism swept across America during those years. Images of Uncle Sam, the stars and stripes, minutemen, and soldiers who were on the front lines, such pictures were everywhere. Although their country had turned its back on their rights, the vast majority of Nikkei inside the ten War Relocation Authority (WRA) camps considered themselves loyal Americans and did what they could to prove it. In Heart Mountain, scouts were selling defense stamps and collecting scrap for the war effort.

Dec 3, 1942

I didn't write yesterday because I went to see the movies and didn't get home 'til late. Sonja Heine & John Payne in "Sun Valley Seranade." It was pretty good. After seeing that picture I (just ran out of ink) wish I could ski. (Say it looks like this ink is of different shade.) Well I better get to bed every one is waiting for me to turn the light off.

SEES MOVIE?

Turning the lights off at night was a recurrent tension in the Hayamis' crowded barrack. Their so-called "apartment" was nothing more than a single room for six people with one bare bulb hanging overhead. Family members hung sheets or blankets between their cots for privacy, but if the light was on for one person, it was on for everyone.

Going to the movies was a welcome change from everyday life. The two theatres, the Pagoda and the Dawn, were nothing like the movie palaces in California. Basically they were simply barracks with folding chairs. Ticket cost a dime for adults and a nickel for children. Newsreels gave them glimpses of the world outside and films, however old, allowed for some entertaining escapism. Frank wrote that movies were shown once a week, but he complained . . .

Our leisure time was very dull . . . a full time recreation director tried to maintain inmate morale by providing as much entertainment as he could recruit from whatever talent was available in the camp. One notable entertainer was a professional juggler who spun dishes on the end of wands, much to the amazement of viewers. There were Japanese dancers and singers, Hawaiian bands, singers, Japanese type theatrical presentations, and other forms of entertainment.

Frank Hayami letter to Mike Mackey, Oct. 16, 1992

Dec. 4, 1942

Brr. Was it cold today! The mercury hovered around between 0° and 20°.

Dec. 5, 1942

Played football in the morning and listened to football games in the after-noon. P.S. Frank isn't mad at me no more. He offered me some apple cider.

Dec. 6, 1942

Went to Sunday School and studied or messed around most of the rest of the day.

Gosh it's cold around here! When I was back home about the coldest it ever got was 29° above. It was down to about 5 below here this morning. Oh well. Its not so cold. The announcer on the radio from LA just said that he envied us back East, we will have a White Xmas. Heck I envy him more. Wish I were back home to see a nice green Xmas not a white Xmas.

The temperature was to plunge even lower in the weeks ahead, down to a record minus 28 degrees. The cold was especially harsh for those living in flimsy barracks with coal shortages, inadequate insulation, and few winter clothes. It was a bitter time with no way of knowing what might happen next.

December 7th would never again be just another day in December. Memories of that fateful day in 1941 would return to haunt Americans for generations to come. These are Stan's entries, just a year after the attack on Pearl Harbor, when the pain of what followed was still very fresh . . . .

Stan's dramatic drawing of December 7th was the frontispiece of the annual, Tempo.

Dec. 7, 1942

Today was the day last year in which this whole mess started. Last year it was Sunday.

I was busy outside that morning so I didn't hear about it when it hap-pened. However in the afternoon business slowed down to a stand still, not a customer came for about an hour so I went back to the house and turned on the radio. The announcer kept butting in. "Attention to all men in service.

Report at once to your station. All leaves cancelled." Then tuning in on a news broadcast I heard the stunning news. "Pearl Harbor bombed!!" "About fifty planes came over the harbor at etc." I turned off the radio and rushed out front and told pa & ma.

That night we all felt as if we were ... still having a nightmare. Obasan called and told about what was happening in L.A. That night we all went to sleep wondering what was going to happen to us. Little did I know then that one year from then I would be in Heart Mountain Wyo. in a evacuation camp.

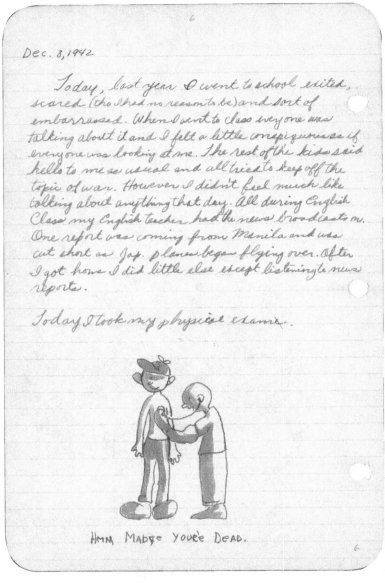

Dec. 8. 1942

Today, last year I went to school exited, scared (tho I had no reason to be) and sort of embarrassed. When I went to class everyone was talking about it and I felt a little conspiquous as if everyone was looking at me. The rest of the kids said hello to me as usual and all tried to keep off the topic of war. However I didn't feel much like talking about anything that day. All during English class my English teacher had the news broadcasts on. One report was coming from Manila and was cut short as Jap. planes began flying over. After I got home I did little else except listening to the news reports.

Today I took my physical exam.

Stan's brother Walt remembers December 7th this way . . .

It was a Sunday and in the nursery business, Saturdays and Sundays were the busiest days. But all of a sudden the business stopped and I went inside. My brother and I were both football fanatics so we turned on the radio to listen to the game and it was . . . what should I say . . . it was traumatic.

I remember my mom and dad had to go sign up as alien residents. And my uncle was taken away immediately by the FBI. He was a big car dealer and he was influential in the community. He entertained dignitaries when they came from Japan. So that left my aunt alone. She was my dad's sister. She asked that we move in with her in LA. I guess we had to get permission to do that, but we moved and it was there that we got the orders to leave. That's the reason we ended up in Heart Mountain. Otherwise we would have ended up in Poston."

Walter Hayami interview with author, Nov. 4, 2004

The Hayami family was at least together. The Hayamis had worked hard to make a new life in California. In the '30s they rented an orchard that they eventually bought in their American children's names, since Issei could not legally own land. Now they feared all was lost. There were few choices. Walt remembers that his dad turned his nursery over to a neighbor with an agreement that the neighbor would return the nursery with an equal inventory when they returned or pay five cents on every can in their inventory of plants. It was not a good deal, but the only deal his dad could make.

While adults struggled with losing the fruits of their long years of back-breaking labor, their children suffered their own childish losses. Many still recall the ache of leaving the only home they had ever known, of being treated as outcasts by schoolmates and teachers, of pets that had to be given away or worse. Walter Hayami, then 13 years old, remembers it this way . . .

I was addicted to comic books and I would ask if I could buy one almost every day. When we were about to leave, my friend LeRoy tells me we made an agreement that I would send him money and he would send me comic books . . .and apparently it worked for awhile. I don't really remember this agreement, but I got a phone call from LeRoy about three years ago, he looked me up on the Internet. Anyway, he says he had something he wanted to talk to me about. In fact it had been bothering him ever since

I left. This is sixty years later! According to LeRoy we made an agreement that he would send me comic books and I would send him the money. But, he told me that his mother found out about it and another mother said he should stop because it was unpatriotic!

Walter Hayami interview with author, Nov. 4, 2004

Was Walt puzzled when the comics stopped coming? He doesn't really remember. He did know that he didn't have any money to speak of—nobody did. So he couldn't have kept his part of the bargain. From time to time, he was able to buy a comic and Walt recalls that even Stan would read them . . .as Stan put it, "If you are going to buy them I am going to read them."

Dec. 12, 1942

Sorry I did not write the last night or so, it is because I was studying for my Chemistry test.

Tomorrow at Los Angeles U.C.L.A. plays U.S.C. to determine who goes to the Rose bowl. Gosh I wish I were home so I could see that game. Oh well it's going to be some game anyway. Bill Stern is going to broadcast that game. I hope UCLA wins. If they win and if they go to the Rose Bowl it'll be the first time they will go.

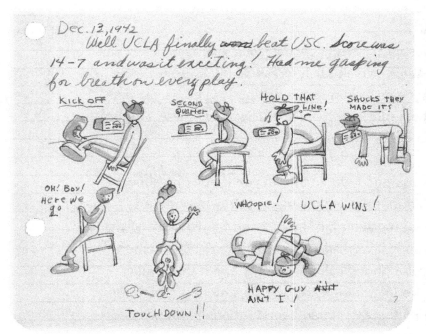

Dec. 13, 1942

Well UCLA finally won beat USC. Score was 14–7 and was it exciting! Had me gasping for breath on every play.

Each of the ten War Relocation Authority camps had a newspaper. Events that happened in one were frequently reported to the others – even if the news was slightly delayed. A year after the war began, while most of the country devoted December 7, 1942 to parades, bond drives, wreaths, speeches, and other "Remember Pearl Harbor!" celebrations, Stan was shocked to read about the events at Manzanar, another WRA camp in the eastern part of California, outside the declared "military" zone . . .

Dec. 14, 1942

Last Monday (Dec. 7) the isseis and kibeis rioted at Manzanar. They were celebrating Pearl Harbor and some loyal American niseis tried to stop them and they (rioters) killed one and injured several others. Among those that were injured and had to be taken away for his safety was Tad Uyeno. Tad lived across the street from us at San Gabriel and was our competitor. The internal police could do nothing so the Military Police were summoned into camp. The rioters charged the MPs with rocks so they threw tear bombs. When this didn't work they shot the rioters and wounded a few. Now Manzanar is under Marshall martial law. During the riot in which there was a mob of about 4,000, one group tried to haul down the "stars and stripes" but failed as fourteen boy scouts stood guard with rocks and repulsed them.

I hope nothing like that happens around here. Now the politicians and such are starting all over again in trying to take Jap American citizenship away and make things more strict in camp. Heck those guys should remember that over half are loyal Americans and the rest are kibeis and isseis. I don't see why inocent and good guys have to pay for stuff that the Japanese do. Things like what happened at Manzanar make all of us look like bad saboteurs when just a minority are the ones causing trouble. Darn it anyhow us loyal Jap. American's have no chance. When we're outside people look at us suspiciously and think we're spies. Now that we're in camp the Japs look at us and say we're bad because we still love America. And now the people outside want to take our citizenship away from us as if we're the bad ones, when it's really the kibeis and isseis. If they take our citizenship away from us we'll be people without a country, 'cause, gee whiz! who in the hell wants a Japanese citizenship. I wouldn't go there for nothin'. I guess if they take our citizenship I'll just have to sneak off to some little island and start my own country.

P.S. Tonight we had a twenty minute blackout.

When Stan refers to the Kibei he is talking about American born Nisei who were sent to Japan to be educated and then returned to the USA. As a result of having spent time in Japan they were often suspected of being pro-Japanese. Stan was making a sweeping generalization when he seems to say that all Issei or Kibei were anti-American. In fact, most Issei considered America their adopted home and the home of their children. The Kibei considered themselves American—and many found their years in Japan difficult due to the cultural differences.

Stanley attributes the riot in Manzanar solely to the anniversary of Pearl Harbor, but in fact, other issues had been brewing. There was unrest towards camp guards and administrators and a festering anger at the Japanese American Citizens League (JACL), a group of mostly college educated Nisei that had supported going along peacefully to the camps, instead of standing firm for their civil liberties.

With few exceptions, the Issei, Kibei, and Nisei went into the camps without protest. After the attack on Pearl Harbor the country was united in the cause of defending America. Going into the camps was considered by some the only way show their patriotism, although many resented being forced to give up their constitutionally guaranteed freedoms based solely upon racial suspicion. Once inside, there was growing anger and frustration as people reflected on their terrible losses, their miserable living conditions, and the restrictions under which they were forced to live. They naturally looked for others to blame for their circumstances. Stanley's suspicion of the Issei and Kibei reflects the kind of divisions that the incarceration created between groups.

The politicians Stan refers to in his diary were not satisfied that the Nikkei were imprisoned. Getting the Nikkei out of California was just the first part of their bigger dream, to deport all the Nikkei from the United States permanently. They not only attacked the Issei, the pressure was on to take away the citizenship of the Nisei, Stan's generation. This form of Nativism was neither unique nor new. There were anti-Mexican groups operating at the same time. Minority students often went to de-facto segregated schools on the West Coast, just as African American children went to segregated schools in the South. Years earlier there had been a "Chinese Must Go!" movement. In 1941, war with Japan provided the perfect political climate for bringing long simmering racism to a boil. Not only were the Nikkei imprisoned, if all went well, the Nativists would have every last Nikkei shipped back to Japan.

That winter one of the avid anti-Nikkei groups, the Native Sons of the Golden West, brought a lawsuit to strip the Nisei of their citizenship. For Stan and others of his generation the threat was real. A year earlier, no one would have believed the Nikkei would be locked away in a concentration camp in Wyoming. If this could happen, what else might follow?

Stan is now well aware of the problems outside, but, Stan being Stan, in his typical style continued to work on the smaller problems—ones that he could do something about solving.

Dec. 16, 1942

Man did my algebra teacher give us some tough problems. She gave us ten to do and I only did two. Those two took me three hours to do.

Dec. 17, 1942

Well those problems didn't turn out so tough as all that. Today in Algebra class I did the rest. Had a Spanish test today, boy was it hard!

Gosh when a guy is busy as I am, I'm taking five subjects, he wishes he could take or do more, but when he's doing nothing to keep busy he doesn't feel like doing anything. Like me, right now I have all I can handle right now, but I wish I could take more and read and do more.

Dec. 19, 1942

Wonder what to get Papa for X'mas.

Dec 21, 1942

Darn it, looks as if I done went and caught a cold. Seems as if last year around this time I had a cold.

Well no school for the next few days or so. X'mas holidays.

Tried to make some X'mas cards, but most were no good. Don't think I'll send any.

Dec. 24, 1942

Doggone it! yesterday was my birthday and I didn't even know it. Today I was saying that it'll be two years more before I sign up for the draft, when Sach says "what do you mean you're seventeen now." So I'm seventeen now. I don't feel like it. I mean I don't feel grown up like some people who are seventeen. Some are already out in the Pacific or someplace fighting.

Yesterday night I got a X'mas present from someone I don't even know. I got it from a lady named Mrs. C.W. Evans who lives way over in Minominee, Michigan. I got the present via the Sunday School. Lot of other kids got presents, too. Walter, George and Tomo. Their presents came from all over the country. Walt's came from New York. Tomo's came from New Mexico. And George's came from Minnesota. Besides the presents everybody in the camp under nineteen gets a present whether they go to Sunday school or not. All the presents sent to this camp were sent by the Presbyterian Union Church. I really think it was a fine gesture. I'm going to write to the lady as soon as I can.

Church groups all over the United States were encouraged to send gifts for the Japanese American children. However, staunch racists groups that opposed any kindness to the Nikkei scorned these acts of kindness. Angry letters to the editors and cartoons about the gifts expressed hatred of the Nikkei and attacked those who sent gifts.

Dec 25, 1942

Merry Xmas! Well I hoped for a White Christmas and tonight it snowed. This morning I went to church then went to Nishiokas house with Walt, Tomo, George, and a bunch of other guys. We played a game of cards and Nishioka's mother served us cocoa, cake, candy, and soup. When we left at around 2 'clock  *we were so full we could hardly move. Walt and I went home and got our coats, because it was beginning to get a little chilly, and then we went to see the football game. The game was between Pomona and Santa Anita which ended in a 6 to 6 tie.*

After the game we came home and at four o'clock we had a nice turkey dinner, yum, yum!!

At about 7:00 o'clock I went to our mess hall Xmas party. It was lots of fun! We played some games, one of which I had to eat crackers and then whistle. I couldn't even eat one of the five crackers. Walt, Frank and Dick Tomemura sang and played some Hawaiian songs. Dick was a homesick sailor from Hawaii who got caught in the states when the war began.

After the games and entertainment Santa Claus came, much to the delight and happiness of the kids. George's little sister Sachie was so scared when she saw Santa that she cried.

Masoa and Tadao, and some other little kids went up to shake hands with Santa and get some candy and nuts from him. They looked as if they were in a trance. They came back holding up their package and looking intently at it. Then they showed them to everybody. Then they dragged out big boxes filled with presents for everybody. Walter got a book and some socks. (Oh that reminds me Sach gave me four pairs of dress socks. She also gave Frank, Pa, Ma and Walt socks. I gave Frank and Pa stationery and oranges. To ma I gave five balls of crocheting [yarn]. The presents I'm giving to Sach and Walt haven't come yet.*

Gifts came from church groups all over the country and were given to everyone under 17.

I'm giving Sach a stamp book and to Walt a glider. I got a bottle of cologne from a woman in S. Dakota. Well thats about all now. Except that I didn't expect much of this Xmas and instead I [had] about the most fun that I ever had.

In his next entry Stan is not too eager to return to school. It seems vacations ended too soon, even in 1942.

Dec. 26, 1942

Shucks already its Saturday night. Monday it's back to school.

Didn't do much all day today. Just played some football and watched some football and thats about all.

It was plenty cold today, right now the temperature is zero.

Miss Hudson, who was my English teacher back home, sent me a box of Sees candy. I think that was really nice of her. Gosh I got presents from people I didn't know & candy from my teacher, gee I don't see how I deserve it.

I use some of that cologne today. Do I smell good! I let George use some of it and he put it on his hair.

Gifts from outside were the only gifts that many children in the camps would receive that year. Families inside the camps had limited funds. Even those with regular jobs earned less than sixty cents a day, leaving little for gifts other than things one really needed. For Stanley and those inside the camps the gifts from strangers were tokens that said they were not forgotten.

Dec. 27, 1942

Let's see now what did I do today. Well I went to Sunday school in the morning and played football in the afternoon. Guess that's about all I did.

I was just listening to John B. Hughs. He talked about post war planning and the reason why we must win the peace as well as the war. Which reminds me of an article I have read previously about that subject. One was by Louis Adamic, he says to start training immigrants and their American offspring for the reconstruction and leadership of war torn countries. He says to follow Pearl S. Bucks suggestion of sending Niseis like us in relocation centers to Japan after the war in leading the Japanese to a more democratic way of government. I wonder if it would work? One question problem is that the Japanese have an entirely different set of ideals to the niseis' American ideals. It would take a long time to change this.

There is an underlying problem in this idea for postwar leadership that obviously bothered Stan. Pearl Buck, a greatly admired Nobel prize winning novelist, did not seem to understand that American born Nisei were not raised in the traditions of their Japanese ancestors. Nisei like Stan felt little kinship to the people of Japan who believed in the Emperor as a living god.

Just now on the radio, I heard a broadcast by a commentator, of a Nisei, who immediately after the war started joined the army. He was sent to Australia as an interpreter under General Mac Arthur. Soon he became tired of being a soldier with a pen, so he asked for a gun and permission to be sent into battle. At first they refused him because of the double danger he faces. He would be shot by the Japanese and because of his face he might be shot by his own men. Because of his persistence however they sent him to the battle zone. They assigned an American as a bodyguard to lessen the danger, but the danger he faces is still great. So tonight in some jungle he is risking his life, so he can teach his parents people a lesson, and punish them for what they did. I don't know this certain nisei soldier, but I feel proud of him and what he is doing. He is showing that nisei are loyal Americans.

Stan writes about the Nisei soldier with great admiration. At the time this was written, the U.S. Army had turned away Japanese Americans who tried to enlist. Right after Pearl Harbor, most Nisei who were already in the service were discharged or given menial jobs. Soon after December 7th, all Nisei who were previously classified as 1-A, and qualified to serve in the army, were reclassified as 4-C, as enemy aliens! They did not consider themselves as the enemy—nor were they aliens.

To Stan, the young soldier in Mac Arthur's headquarters represented the "honor" of many Nisei. In fact, thousands of Nisei became interpreters and translators in the Military Intelligence Service (MIS) although the full extent of their role in the war was not generally known until many years later. It's clear, Stan has a sense of pride in the courage and patriotic actions of this young man.

P.S. Frankie Nishioka's mother gave me some packages of dehydrated soup. I really love soup. Gee! I wish she wouldn't give me so much. I don't like to be obligated. The reason she gives them to me is because I helped Frankie with his geometry a few times. Gosh! The next time I'll have to make Frankie promise not to give me anything when I help him.

Stan's reaction to the generosity of Frankie's mom is what many Nikkei would laughingly call, "so Japanesie." Thanking others is an expected courtesy that is often accompanied with a gift to reciprocate. But Stan has no way to return the gift and he is embarrassed to simply accept something without giving some token in return.

Dec. 28, 1942
Sorry haven't anytime to write today either.

Dec 30, 1942
The reason I didn't write the last few days was because I had to go to parties. Last night our homeroom had a party. It turned out OK but not so good.

Next time we have a party I'll have to plan it better.

Tonight I went to our Sunday school party. It was a lotta fun! We had good refreshments too.

After the party I went to our mess hall and watched them making mochie. Pa & Frank are helping. I think they have to stay up until about 4:00 o'clock tomorrow morning.

Mochi is a very special treat; sweet rice cakes traditionally eaten on the New Year. In ancient times rice was a special food that was eaten only on special occasions. Each grain of rice was considered a "human soul" and the pounded rice represented millions of souls. Mochi takes hours of preparation and strong arms as the cooked rice is pounded with a wooden mallet. Pounding the rice was thought to give one time to reflect on the previous year and think of the future. After the rice is pounded to a paste, sweetened flour is added. Then the mochi is hand shaped into small cakes.

In his next entries Stan reflects on the past year and worries about what will happen next . . .

Dec 31, 1942

Well today is the last day of 1942. The band is playing in our mess hall tonight for the dance.

Well a lot of things happened this year. Most weren't very good, but maybe the things that happened will have been for the better in the end.

Well pa is mad and wants me to go to sleep so good nite until next year.

1943

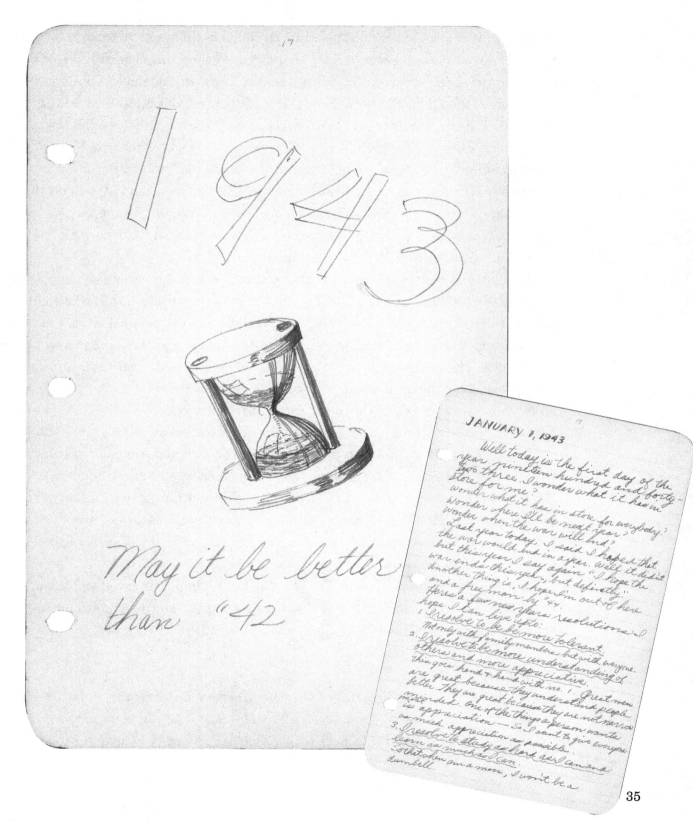

1943

May it be better than "42

JANUARY 1, 1943

Well today is the first day of the year, nineteen hundred and forty-two three. I wonder what it has in store for me? I wonder what it has in store for everybody? I wonder where I'll be next year. I wonder when the war will end?

Last year today, I said I hoped that the war would end in a year. Well it didn't but this year I say again "I hope the war ends this year," but definitely." Another thing is, I hope I'm out of here and a free man by "44.

Here's a few new years resolutions I hope I can live up to:
1. I resolve to be be more tolerant. Not only with family members, but with everyone.
2. I resolve to be more understanding of others and more appreciative. They goes hand + hand with no. 1. Great men are great because they understand people better. They are great because they are not narrow minded. One of the things a person wants is appreciation — so I want to give everyone as much appreciation as possible.
3. I resolve to study as hard as I can and learn as much as I can. So that when am a man, I won't be a dumbell.

1943

Almost all of Stanley's diary entries focus on two very different subjects. Most often he writes about personal concerns for his grades in school, his own abilities, or his doubts about them. What will he do with his life? How will he make a difference? What career should he choose? When he is not writing about himself he writes about much more global issues. He's concerned with world affairs—he follows the war news and frequently speculates on what will happen after the war. Yet, aware as he is, Stanley almost never writes about the political climate in the camp.

He says little about issues that stirred conflict between the Nikkei and the WRA administrators or between Nikkei groups that did not always see eye to eye. It is almost as if such troubles were too intense to deal with, so with few exceptions, Stanley avoids writing about them.

In early 1943, after the shock of the evacuation and the wretched conditions of the assembly centers, the Nikkei settled as best they could into the relocation camps. In Heart Mountain there were not enough stoves installed or coal to heat the barracks. Supplies of food, warm winter coats, and school equipment were inadequate. The rush to incarcerate the Nikkei was so swift that the camps were not prepared for the basic needs of those who were imprisoned.

Late in January, the government served up two new bombshells that went off almost at the same time. After rejecting the Nisei as "enemy aliens" in 1942, the army called for volunteers for a segregated all-Nisei combat team. At the same time everyone inside the camps who was 17 or older, was required to answer a "loyalty" questionnaire that set off conflicts within families as well as between groups and the administration. In the coming months the issues of army volunteers and the related "loyalty" questionnaire became the most disturbing events since the Nikkei had been forced to leave their homes.

Although Stanley mentions some of these events in passing, you would not know from reading his diary that these were among the stormiest days for the Nikkei community in Heart Mountain and all the other WRA camps.

January 1, 1943

Well today is the first day of the year nineteen hundred and forty three. I wonder what it has in store for me? Wonder what it has in store for everybody? Wonder where I'll be next year? Wonder when the war will end?

Last year today I said I hope the war would end in a year. Well, it didn't but this year I say again "I hope the war ends this year, but definitely." Another thing is I hope I'm out of here and a free man by '44.

Here's a few new year's resolutions I hope I can live up to.

I resolve to be more tolerant.

Not only with family members but with everyone.

I resolve to be more understanding of others and more appreciative . . . this goes hand in hand with no. 1. *Great men are great because they understand people better. They are great because they are not narrow-minded. One of the things a person wants most is appreciation—So I want to give everyone as much appreciation as possible.*

I resolve to study as hard as I can and learn as much as I can. So that when I am a man, I won't be a dumbbell.

I resolve to help Ma and Pa more.

I resolve not to abandon my high school ambitions.

Prediction: War will end between 1944–1945. About 1½ years more.

Today in the morning I played cards, and in the afternoon I listened to football games. Well the rose

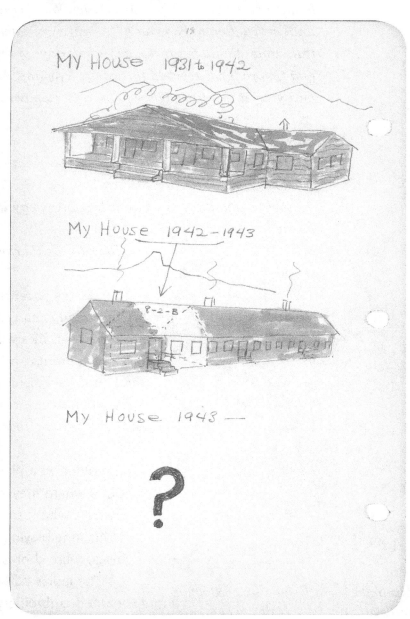

bowl game came out as expected but not as I hoped. Most people said that Georgia would smother U.C.L.A. but I said it would be pretty close. U.C.L.A. held Georgia scoreless for three quarters, but Georgia poured it on in the last and won 9-0. I hoped U.C.L.A. would win, which they didn't however.

Last year at this time, I was at home in San Gabriel, Calif. And today I'm far away in an evacuation camp here in Heart Mountain, Wyo. Gosh, a lot happened last year. In the spring we had to work hard to sell our stock. At Easter we quit, handed over the nursery to Mr. Dailey. We moved to Los Angeles for a month until evacuation to Pomona A. [Assembly] Center. After Pomona we boarded a train and after about three and a half days of traveling through Nevada, Utah, and Colorado we reached this camp Wyoming. And here I am today hoping that next year at this time, I'll be home or someplace else outside of camp.

Jan. 2, 1943

Tonight I saw my first movie in two months or so. The picture was "Hoosier Boy" played by Mickey Rooney. I don't know how old the movie is but it must be about 3 years old at least. Anyway it was good. It was Mama's first movie in about ten years.

Tonight the thermometer shows 14° below zero.

Life in the barrack was a crowded affair. A curtain was the only way to have privacy in a one-room "apartment."

For Stan's parents, life in Heart Mountain brought many changes. Before the war Mama would not have been likely to go to the movies. Like most Issei, his parents spoke Japanese. Movies in English would not have been too entertaining. Traditional forms of entertainment continued to be of interest as Frank's letter recalled . . .

The older men played a form of Japanese chess, GOH, where they were able to play against GOH masters who were in camp. My father spent most of his time playing GOH when he wasn't busy with his coal-fire chores.

The ladies had their craft classes where they learned embroidery, sewing, dancing, and flower arrangement. My mother was very active in all of these classes. She especially enjoyed embroidery and English classes. She really had a good time at the English classes where the ladies had a real raucous time laughing at each others attempts to pronounce difficult English words.

Frank Hayami letter to Mike Mackey, Oct. 16, 1992

Perhaps it was the English class that changed Mrs. Hayami's interest in movies. The WRA offered "Americanization" classes that were designed to prepare the Nikkei for life after camp. What better way to reinforce English and American customs than with movies that mirrored life in small towns and big cities of America? Yet, there had to be a sense of irony in teaching "Democracy" in a prison camp where civil liberties guaranteed by the Constitution were being denied. If there was any positive thing about camp life for the older generation, having time for entertainment was new. After years of work-

Teaching about "Democracy at Work" inside a prison camp.

ing long hours in the nursery and home, Mrs. Hayami now had more time to spend with friends. Still, that was a small comfort compared to the losses she and her family endured as prisoners.

Jan 3, 1943 SUNDAY

Man! its so cold tonight that my hair froze as I was coming back from the shower.

During their first winter in Wyoming, Walt recalls, the temperature dropped to 23 below zero. "We Californians weren't used to that. It was a dry cold, so it wasn't that bad, but if you went to the restroom in the morning and brushed your teeth and combed your hair, by the time you got back the hair in your nostrils was frozen and the hair on your head was stiff."

Stanley did not expend many words on the conditions of their new home. Frank describes the barrack they lived in with these words . . ..

Our living accommodations were very sparse. No running water, no toilet, no baths in our single 20 ft by 24 ft room housing 6 members of our family. The lack of privacy bothered the two female members of our family. This was solved by stringing ropes from the ceiling around their cots, and draping sheets from the rope to the floor creating some privacy. Rags and newspapers were stuffed into the cracks between the tarpaper covered wood siding to keep out the cold. Heat was provided by a coal-burning stove and my father was the self-appointed coal go-fer and stoker of the fire.

Since most of us were from the west coast, the coal stove was a novelty and an unfamiliar appliance. This led to quite a number of stove fires caused by people putting too much coal into the stoves. This caused the stoves to become cherry red and burn themselves into the floor. My father eventually learned to bank the coal leading to a uniform all night fire. The only problem from then on was the availability of coal.

I heard later that some of the other blocks had installed home-made Japanese style deep soaking tubs (furo) made of wood for those desiring a good soak after showering. I think that the greatest discomfort we suffered here was in going to the bathroom through the snow on a very cold freezing Wyoming night.

Frank Hayami letter to Mike Mackey,
Oct. 16, 1992

Each barrack had six one-room "apartments" with a single light and coal-burning stove in each room. A family of 5–8 had a room 24' X 20'; smaller family lived in a room 16' X 20'. There were 30 "blocks"—all exactly the same. Each block had 24 barracks, in rows of six. Between the rows were service buildings—a mess hall and an H-shaped structure with a boiler room, a laundry room, and two latrines. The other half block was a mirror image. Between the halves there was a firebreak and two recreation halls. An open space was used for softball and basketball.

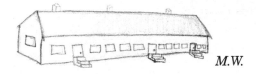

M.W.

40

Jan 4, 1943

This week is going to be full of tests. English Test tomorrow will start the ball rolling. All I hope is that I get good grades in all of them—thats all.

Next semester I'm going to enroll in an art class. Gee-that'll be six subjects I'm going to have to take. Most I ever took was five subjects plus gym.

Around summer we are probably going to have to make a decision on whether to stay in camp or move to some middle western community. If we do decide to go out I wonder which town we will go to. I think we should go to a town where there are no Japanese. If too many Japanese go to one town, people will begin to dislike us. Denver is getting so there are too many Japanese. There were only 200 before evacuation and now there are 800.

From the start there were opportunities for the Heart Mountaineers to leave on temporary or permanent leave. Workers were desperately needed to harvest sugar beets, potatoes, and other crops. In Iowa, Montana, and Wyoming, young men who used to work their family farms had left for the army or work in defense plants. Many Nisei boys took their places, working for short periods of time on farms and then returning to camp.

Other Nisei who could find more permanent employment were able to go to towns and cities in the Mid-west and East if they had clearance from the FBI. Not too many people applied for such leaves, since few had any place to go; and they had legitimate concerns about how they would be accepted.

Soon all of that would change. The pressure to leave would become great.

Inside the schools, older students, like Stanley, were urged to encourage their families to leave or to allow them to leave on their own. The camp newspaper, the Heart Mountain Sentinel, ran a contest, looking for a winning essay by a student on "Why We Should Relocate." Stan's desire to go someplace where there were not a lot of Nikkei mirrors what the WRA was telling them. The administration was urging them to avoid living in close-knit communities: to settle in communities where one or two families might be assimilated—or at least not seem a threat.

Leaving the camps was a frightening prospect, especially for the older generation, who'd lost the security they'd worked so hard to accumulate before the war. Forced to leave their homes and businesses on short notice, these were people with bitter memories of selling their cherished property at a loss and walking away with next to nothing. Despite the hardships and the loss of liberty the camps represented, they did provide a type of security against a strange new world where the Nikkei were not sure of being welcome. Young adults, being more adventurous and less experienced were generally the first ones to leave. For the Issei and those with younger children, life inside was the only real choice.

For now, school continued to be Stanley's greatest concern. His belief in the importance of education was not just something he heard from his teachers. His Issei parents had instilled this idea, expecting their children to do well in school. Education was the key to the better life they had worked so hard to achieve. Children of immigrants were expected to become assimilated as Americans. This "melting pot" mentality was true of immigrants from Europe as well as Asia. They were pressured to throw off ties to the past, to give up language and traditions of the old world and embrace the new, to become 100% American. For Asian Americans, with their distinctive ethnic features, it was harder to disappear into the mainstream of white America. Yet most of Stanley's generation thought of themselves as exactly that—Americans. And in school they learned to believe in the Constitution. Before the war they did not believe that their government would ever treat them as anything but American citizens.

Inside the camp young people held fast to their patriotic beliefs, mixed with some doubts. As they saluted the flag in school each day, the words "liberty and justice for all" were like an irritating pebble in a shoe—"liberty and justice for some" was closer to the truth. When a new flagpole was dedicated that January, the school principal worried that students might not show up. But Student Body President Ted Fujioka assured him the students would be there and they were. Somewhere in that picture, it's likely that Stan is saluting the new flag.

If he did well in school, Stan could look forward to college and the future. But not meeting his own expectations for high grades seems to be a source of constant disappointment.

Flag Salute, 1943. Photograph by Hansel Mieth.

Jan. 6, 1943

Man! I'm going to have four tests tomorrow! I've only had one so far. That's English.

42

Jan 7, 1943

I had three tests today. I thought I was going to have an Algebra test but I didn't. I didn't do very good in any of my tests. In Chem. test we had ten probs [problems] & I think I missed two. Spanish test was really horrible. I must have missed about 20 pts. Well its 10:20 so I better go to bed.

Well hello again, I didn't go to sleep yet. Pa & Ma & Frank are talking about our next-door neighbor who got thrown into jail tonight. He was making sake [fermented rice wine] in the mess hall.

Jan 8, 1943

Last night I had to go to sleep without writing so this morning I'm writing to make up. Last night I wrote to my former teacher Miss Hudson thanking her for my sending me a box of candy and telling her of the Xmas that I had. So that reminds me of the story my Sunday school teacher Yosh Kodama told us, which really makes me feel ashamed of myself.

Far away in New Mexico in an isolated spot, there are a few very poor Mexicans who attended a certain Mission. There poor people were told by the priest that the kids in Heart Mountain wouldn't have a very good Christmas this year, because they didn't have an income, and because they were uprooted from their homes and put into camp. Well these people were poor themselves but they wanted to help us anyway. They went to their priest and said that they didn't have much money and the nearest store was about fifty miles away, what could they do? The priest answered by going to that store and buying some gifts and bringing them back. He exchanged these gifts for chickens, vegetables and such that they could spare and took these back to the store in exchange for the gifts. I think that I'll remember this forever.

Today in History class our teacher discussed our situation with us. She says that as a whole the general public doesn't know us and thinks we are all bad. She warns that if we go out for private relocation not to go where there are already too many Japanese, because we would then tend to be conspicuous and would be hated all the worse. But instead she suggests that we go to some small town where no Japanese live, because then the community will get to know us as individuals. She also says that she thinks we got a raw deal. She doesn't see where German and Italian aliens are more [less?] dangerous than Jap. American citizens.

This idea of disappearing into the mainstream became a constant mantra of the War Relocation Authority (WRA). Before the war, those who lived in cities such as Los Angeles, San Francisco, San Diego, and San Jose tended to be ghettoized. This was true of all poor immigrant groups. As strangers in a new land, ethnic groups found comfort in living with those who shared the same language and culture. But realistically, living in such ethnic neighborhoods was not a matter of choice. It often had more to do with low rents and acceptance. However, not all the Nikkei came from such crowded urban settings. Those who had farmed often lived in isolation from other Nikkei and their Caucasian neighbors as well. For them, life in the camps came as a shock. More than one would say, "I had never seen so many Japanese people!"

Now, in 1943, the government was saying that the "Little Tokyos" and "Japantowns" should not be re-established. The Nikkei should not recreate ethnic communities, but rather spread themselves thin, where they would not be so noticeable.

In a brochure handed out to those Nikkei who were leaving, a list of "helpful hints for success" urged them not to speak Japanese in public, don't gang up in large groups, don't patronize honky tonks, night clubs, bars, and other such places that reflect unfavorably on all Japanese Americans, don't be conspicuous. Make friends with non-Japanese.

> **The public is slow to recognize your status as an American . . .keep this in mind when prejudice and discriminations hurt you. Always remember your ultimate desire, a free and equal life in America. To attain it may require sacrifices on your part during these trying times.**
>
> *Minidoka Memo to Resettlers, JANM*

In the years that followed the Japanese American community never re-established the urban centers as they existed in the past. Just as the camps did their part in breaking down the unity of the family, the WRA did its part in dividing the Nikkei community.

Jan 9, 1943

Did practically nothing today. In the morning I walked with Jimmy Yada & James Nokada to the clinic so Jimmie should have his lip examined. We waited two hours before we found out the doctors weren't there. In the afternoon I watched some kids in Block 1 ice skate and visited Polito, gee he's getting big. cute too!

I carved half a set of chess in Pomona and I don't feel like making the rest so I'm going to make it into a necklace for Sach.

Jan. 10, 1943

Tonite in the shower room I was talking to a friend of mine and he seems to have quite a defeated attitude. He says, "why study, theres no future here."

Polito is the son of Alice and Paul Nakadate. Alice Fujioka Nakadate was Stan's cousin.

I answer, "yeah, but how about when you get out of here."

He says, "Get out of here? When? I'm too dumb to go to college, and the war will last "till I'm an old man."

Then I say "yes but if you have enough ambition you could probably get out this summer, and besides the government doesn't want to keep all of us here and spend a lot of money on us."

He says, "Oh yeah, they're going to make us raise a lot of crops here so that we can take care of ourselves."

By this time I was thru dressing so before I left I says "Well anyhow I'm not planning on living here all my life!"

In fact, both Stan and his friend were partially right. There were some racists who would have been more than happy to send all the Japanese Americans back to Japan or stick them permanently on isolated reservations like the Native Americans. There were also others, like the American Friends Service Committee that organized the National Japanese American Student Relocation Council to help the Nisei find colleges in the Mid-west and East so that they could leave the camps and continue their education. Stanley bought into the hope of leaving and studying was the ticket.

Traditional Japanese entertainment appealed to the Issei, not to Nisei like Stan.

Tonight Walt, George, & Tomo are in the mess hall seeing a program for the issei. They say "Well maybe they'll

45

give us something to eat afterwards."

Heck! I've got a lot more to write but everyone else is sleeping already so I'd better turn off the lights so they can sleep better. So tomorrow I write about what I think about post war planning and about a World Federal Government.

"Stan and Walt: fish and beans"

A candid photo of Walt, Stan and their mother in the mess hall.

Imagine Walt and his pals sitting through a program designed for the Issei, the old folks, on the chance of getting something to eat. The topic of food is never far from the minds of boys like Walt who tended to be hungry all the time. In the early days at Heart Mountain, before meal tickets were needed, groups of boys often ran from one mess hall to another trying to get whatever they could to eat.

Frank remembers the mess halls this way:

Each block of tar-papered shacks within the camp had two mess-halls, and two laundry/shower facilities. Within the mess hall, were tables made of two by fours and similar benches. To enter the mess hall one had to show a pass which I believe was punched by a ticket-taker at the door. Then you filed by the counter where your plate was served with food and you found yourself a table.

You knew the food was bad when the waitresses came around asking if you wanted seconds . . . speaking of bad foods, one of the worst meals we had at Heart Mountain was the days we were served slabs of fat at the main meal. After one bite, I pushed it aside and ate the remaining food on my plate, rice. When I mentioned it to my Caucasian administrator . . . he told me that slabs of pure fat were considered a delicacy in this area. He also told me about another Western gourmet delight, the Rocky Mountain oysters, from which we, fortunately, were spared.

The quality of the meals served at the camps depended a great deal on the skill of the mess-hall cooks recruited from among the inmates. We, on Block 8, had the misfortune of having one of the worse teams in camp. The cooked meals were consistently bad. It was bad enough that the government provided us with rations that were on the low quality side but to have them ruined by amateur cooks was the last straw. At a local block meeting . . . the

46

incumbent cooks were ousted and a new team installed.

The quality of the cooking improved . . .this brings to mind the cooking at block 20 mess-hall, where the cooks were professionals from an outstanding oriental restaurant in the LA area. They took the same ingredients furnished the other mess-halls and turned them into things of delight.

I knew a bunch of guys living on Block 20 who managed to sneak me into their mess-hall after church on Sundays. Every one wanted to take his meals in Block 20 . . . but couldn't get a Block 20 mess-hall ticket.

The waitresses in our mess-hall were quite professional . . .these were older single women, unmarried, who had worked as waitresses in Japanese bar-restaurants (nomiya) urging drinks on men customers. They stood out in our mess hall because they wore heavy make up while the majority of the other women were country women, wives of farmers, with sun-burned leathery faces. Of course, there were wives of merchants or city people who did not have sun-tanned faces. Anyway, these waitresses turned out to be really nice friendly people, much to the relief of the mothers who were concerned about the influence of these women on the sons and husbands.

Stan doesn't have much to say about the food. For Stan the marking period has rolled around once again and he's disappointed. He did not manage to get all As . . .

Wed 13, 1943—Jan.

Sorry I haven't wrote in here for the past few days, but it is because I was so busy. Also today I won't be able to write about what I think about post war planning again.

Today I got my report card. I went down in Algebra, but improved in Chemistry

	This times grades	Last Times grades	Next time?
ENG	A	A	?
History	A	A	?
Alg.	B	A	?
Chem.	A	B	?
Spanish	B	B	?

I hoped they
Would all be A's

Doggone! it any how. I think if I worked a little bit harder I might be able to get all A's. Back home I always got all A's. Of course the competition is harder here.

Jan 14, 1943

Well I guess I'll write today on post war planning and on "World Federal Government" . . . oh, skip post war planning . . . I think I wrote about that before once . . .

Now this World Federal Gov't. idea—I read about it recently in my Scholastic Magazine and men such as Vice President Wallace approve of it. I thought of such a plan about five years before, but I guess these men must of thought of such a plan thirty years ago. In fact I guess about everyone has considered it once before. The plan is to have every nation in the world join in and form just one big nation. It might be called the "United Nations of Earth".

Instead of each nation being an individual, and always disputing over boundries, trade, and such, each nation will merely be a state on the Earth. Each nation will be equal in rights, and each nation will send representatives to the Earth Congress. It will be run as a democracy and the peoples wish shall be the governing factor. Of course, before this system really gets going the people of Earth will have to educate the . . . [unschooled] of India, Africa, and China so that they would be able to take active part in the governing, and be able to raise their standards more nearer the rest of the world.

Now some will say this is impossible—how can those . . . negroes be taught anything? I answer the colored people of Africa probably have as great an intellectual brain as we do—the only thing is they haven't developed it as yet. Look at Dr. Carver, who used to be a slave, and who died recently, with study and an education he became one of the great geniuses of our day. If he was left in Africa he might still be an ignorant savage. So I say it is possible. Another thing is- the colored races of the Earth must overcome the great racial prejudice first—and the rest of the Earth must help.

In many ways, Stan's thinking seems well ahead of his time. In 1943, when he wrote this entry the United Nations did not yet exist. The term "United

Nations," however, was not really new. President Franklin D. Roosevelt coined that name — "Declaration by United Nations" on New Year's Day, 1942, when 26 nations pledged to fight against the Axis.

Long before the war ended students, politicians, and journalists were arguing the merits of an international body of nations, modeled on the failed League of Nations that was unable to prevent World War II. The article in Scholastic that Stan mentions outlines the pros and cons of establishing a "Federal World Government," the hot topic for the National Forensic League debates in high schools that year.

Vice President Henry Wallace, who just a few weeks earlier gave a stirring speech on national radio, titled, World Organization, probably inspired Stanley's ideas as well. Wallace said it would be the height of folly if the United Nations that were fighting the war did not begin planning for the peace. In this speech and other writings, Wallace spoke often of the importance of educating the masses so that they could be productive in what he called the coming "Century of the Common Man."

Stan is very much a young man of his time. His essay reflects a keen awareness of the prevalent racist biases toward minorities, his own and others. He knew from personal experience how far we were, then and now, from attaining the "United Nations of Earth" of his idealistic dreams.

Yet, when he writes about people of color Stanley is ahead of his time. Contrary to the bigotry and public opinion of the time, Stanley believes people of all races have intellectual ability if they are given an education.

When Stanley writes about people of color all over the world, he is not saying he doubts their ability. He is saying the very opposite. His prime example is George Washington Carver, an African American black scientist who was one of Stan's personal heroes. A later entry, on March 25, 1944 goes even further in expressing his sense of admiration and connection to Carver.

Stanley goes on to talk about the problems of communication between people who do not share a common language . . .

Another problem to be met is that of an international language. Some of our present trouble today is caused by language differences. If we had a common language we would be able to understand each other better. I suggest the use of Latin as such. Latin is already used as the universal Scientific language. I wouldn't be at all surprised if in fifty years I was talking Latin to my friends.

One reason I think we will have to have a Federal World Government is to keep from having future wars. The World Government should have a great standing army composed of soldiers from all over the Earth- for the purpose of policing the Earth and keeping everyone in his right place.

Another reason why I think we will have to have this form of gov't is because of the growing smallness of our world. Before the airplane was invent-ed, the earth was comparatively large, but now because of our increased speed of travel, it has become relatively small. And in ten years hence improvements in the airplane will increase speed twice or thrice as much. Perhaps a new mode of travel will be discovered that will make even the airplane obsolete. Then people on Earth will meet others more often and more disagreements will arise. Besides, there will be too much red tape in comparison with the speedy travel What I mean is people will be able to travel to a different country in a fraction of the time it takes to have your passport checked and such. You'll be spending more time going through red tape than traveling.

Well anyway that's just an idea of the "World Federal Gov't."

More than sixty years later we have a less idealized view of the United Nations' ability to step in and stop violence in the far corners of the world. In Stanley's day the ideals of the United Nations offered a war-weary world the great hope of the future. It was the UN that would bring everlasting peace, much as the League of Nations was expected to do after World War I. On the other hand, Stanley accurately predicted that travelers of the future would spend more time going through red tape than traveling!

Stan's thoughts about the "smallness" of the world were probably also inspired by Wallace's speech, in which he said . . .

> Today, measured by travel time, the whole world is actually smaller than was our little country then. When George Washington was inaugurated, it took seven days to go by horse-drawn vehicle from Mount Vernon to New York. Now Army bombers are flown from the United States to China and India in less than three days.

After his long and serious entry Stanley shifts gears suddenly and moves on to the reality of more mundane life.

Right now I'm more concerned about the warm wind we're having that is melting our ice skating rinks up. I ordered some ice skates. I also am worried about my budget which I am just starting. With my $3.75 clothing allowance and .25 from Pa per month I have to buy everything I need.

Jan. 15, 1943

*Today in the **Life** magazine there were some pictures by Grant Wood who died last year around this time. They sure are good.*

My eyes feel tired and have water in them. I think its because I have to study in bad lighting.

Man its cold tonite. Its snowing so hard you can hardly see and wind is blowing like hell.

Jan. 16, 1943

Yike! but it was cold today burrr. It was 12° below zero which was the coldest so far. Once before I think I said that it was 14° below, but we found out later that, that thermometer was wrong. Our present thermometer is right. It'll probably be 20° below tomorrow. And to think, I'll have to get up early tomorrow in order to go to Sunday school.

Jan. 17, 1943

Today I went to Sunday school, as usual, but was it hard getting there. It was so cold (20° below zero) that I bundled up until I looked like an eskimo. James Nokada and I ducked into each laundry house on the way up. However, as soon as I take a hundred steps my eyelids eyelashes would have icicles on them. So when I get to the laundry room I melt the icicles off and keep on going. Anyway I finally got [there]. Hardly anyone was there. After Sunday school, and going back was [not] quite as [hard] as the wind was blowing with us.

For the rest of the day I worked on a picture of myself, which I started last night and finished today. It was the first oil painting I ever did. Its a lot more fun and easier to do than watercolors. I kinda like the picture even if I do say so myself, but I bet in a year, I'll think its quite terrible and cheap looking. Oh well I'll improve.

Jan. 18, 1943

Doggone it! Our room is so noisy that I can't study. There's Tomo, George, Walt, Frank, Sach, Ma and Pa, and the Radio, Guitar, trumpet all in the same room. Oh well I should crab, everyone is entitled to his part in this house. I'm not the only one living in it. Anyhow I'll have to devise a means so I can concentrate better.

Stan frequently mentions the noise of his brother's music that interfered with his studying. It was not just records or the radio. Walt had two buddies who were in the band; one was a trumpet player the other a sax player. Where did they practice? Walt laughed as he confessed they started practicing in the barrack!

I started learning trumpet when we first went to camp. The reason I got a trumpet is my older brother was a guitar player and he was playing in the band and they needed a trumpet player. So he talked my dad into buying me a trumpet. My cousin Eddie had a friend who was a musician in LA, so he sent him the money and he bought me a used trumpet that he mailed to me in camp. At that time the camp wasn't quite full yet, so we used to go up to Block 30, way out in the boon docks. Tomo was my best friend and he was a trumpet player already, so we'd go out in the boon docks and practice.

Eventually I was in the dance band—I played third trumpet—no solos. The leader was George Igawa. He was a tenor sax player. We went out to Powell and other places. I was 14 or 15. We didn't have uniforms, but jackets and slacks and ties. We would play at dances in camp and we were asked to go out to play at war bond rallies. So we went out to play in Powell and in Cody. We didn't have any trouble. They were really receptive. We played all the hit songs of the day . . . "Sentimental Journey," "In the Mood." I know we played in Thermopolis. We used school buses . . . one of the better things about it was they would feed us a real meal! I remember one time we had venison. It was the first time any of us had had that.

Walter Hayami interview with author, Nov. 4, 2004

George Igawa's dance band. Walter is 2nd from the left in the back row.

In late January Stan took up the biggest wintertime activity in Heart Mountain—ice-skating. Below-freezing temperatures made this an ideal sport. For Californians, skating on ice was brand new. Between the upper and lower block there was a big field that was used for baseball in the summer. In the wintertime they filled it with water and that became ice where everyone went skating. All you needed were a pair of skates that were ordered from Sears & Roebuck.

Before this time, most of the kids had only tried roller-skating, but never ice-skating. It was a real thrill! There were figure skates with the ridges on the front and then there were the hockey skates, with pointed blade. Skating seems to inspire Stan's imagination . . .

Ice skating was a popular sport that Stanley enjoyed.

Jan. 23, 1943 Sat. morn.

Last night I wore ice skates for just about the first time. It goes a lot easier than roller skates, but my arches sure hurt! I fell down about 20 times last night, but its still a lot of fun.

Afternoon

I wonder how we will be traveling in the future. Perhaps we will have our own private autogiros and airplanes, which will be able to go to Europe in about a half a day. Perhaps twenty yrs from now the airplane and such will be obsolete, perhaps there will be entirely new traveling methods. Such as rocket ships. Maybe 50 years from now I'll be visiting the moon on afternoons. Maybe we'll be able to be radioed to Europe or Asia in person. Have a sending station which sends your molecules to a receiving station which assembles them in their proper places. Heck if this is impossible how about radio and television, I bet 20 years before they were invented nobody hardly even dreamed of them. Boy some fun I could have, just step into a sending booth, put some slugs into the machine and zip! I'm in Cairo, Egypt or Berlin, Germany (oops wrong number!) P.S. Well maybe I won't be able to get around that fast, but anyway after the war my biggest ambition is to travel around the world.

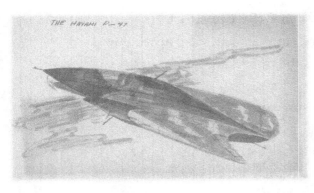

THE HAYAMI P-47

Stanley's 1943 fantasy fighter looks remarkably like a stealth bomber of the 21st century.

It sounds like Stanley was a Trekkie long before Star Trek! He would have totally bought into the adventures as Captain Kirk commanded, "Beam me up, Scottie!"

Jan. 24, 1943 Sunday

Doggone it I did practically nothing this week end. Back at Pomona I made half a chess set and never since had the ambition to finish. It took me a month to do that much. I'm too lazy to finish it and we have a machine made chess set now so I'm going to make it into a necklace for Sach. Thats about all I worked on this weekend.

I just can't seem to study here, its too noisy. I think I have to invent something to wear on my ears that would shut out the noise.

January 25, 1943

Darn it! I got my first F on a test today. First one I ever got! It was on a[n] algebra test. There were 21 problems and I missed 10. 6 of those I missed were purely baby blunders. Wrong signs mostly. Tomorrow we are having another test to try to make up. Heck one reason why others make good grades in our class is because they cheat and look over shoulders & compare answers.

January 26, 1943

Today I took another algebra test and I think that I did even worse.
The radio says that President Roosevelt and Prime Minister [Churchill] met in Casablanca today to discuss war plans.

Jan 28, 1943

I got my algebra paper back today. Doggone! Another "F." Got to do something about that. Maybe do my homework twice will help. The gov't has decided to take niseis from camp and use them in the army. Maybe next year I'll be drafted.

There it is, the first mention of the bombshell that will change Stanley's life and the lives of so many Nisei forever. Stan has buried the biggest news of the

New Year at the end of this last entry. Just a few lines with no words about how he feels about that news.

Jan 30, Sat. 1943

Ho-hum am I lazy. Here Ive gotten 2 "Fs" on my algebra tests and spent the whole day doing nothing.

Stan's problems in school seem to keep growing with each entry. Perhaps the real problems he is struggling with are two major events that aroused both fear and anger for the Nikkei. In January, the government did an about-face, announcing they would now accept Nisei volunteers for a "Japanese Combat Team." At the same time, the Army announced that males of military age would need to answer a questionnaire that proved their loyalty.

To add insult to injury, the WRA then decided that everyone over the age of 17, citizen or not, male or female, would be required to answer the questionnaire, "Application for Leave Clearance" whether they wanted to leave or not. It was ironic that the government would ask people they were treating as prisoners to volunteer for the army or to swear allegiance. Government administrators claimed that signing these questionnaires was simply the first step toward clearing the Nikkei for resettlement in other parts of the country. The whole process came to be known as "Registration."

To the Nikkei of both generations the poorly written questionnaire was frightening. Two questions in particular were most troubling. Question 27 asked if they were willing to serve in the army. For the Nisei, it appeared that in signing "yes" to Question 27 they were automatically volunteering for the army. Further, since most Issei were too old to serve, this was a near impossible question to answer with a yes.

Question 28 asked if they were prepared to foreswear any allegiance to the Emperor. For the Nisei, this was insulting. They had never sworn allegiance to the Emperor! For the Issei, saying "yes" meant giving up their Japanese citizenship while they were not allowed to become naturalized citizens of the United States. A "yes" to Question 28 meant they would be citizens without a country!

For weeks the Nikkei tried to ignore the questionnaire. Finally after a long period of agitation Guy Robertson, the director of Heart Mountain, announced that filling out the questionnaire was not a matter of free choice. It had to be answered.

The Nikkei were assured that they were not automatically volunteering for the service, and Question 28 was changed for the Issei who had to swear they would abide by the laws of the United States and do nothing to damage the war effort.

On February 1, 1943 President Franklin Delano Roosevelt announced the formation of the 442nd Regimental Combat Team. "Americanism" he said, "is not, and never was, a matter of race or ancestry." Ironically, the 442nd was to be a racially segregated unit made up of Japanese Americans. It combined the 100th Infantry Battalion, Japanese-Hawaiian soldiers who had been part of the Hawaiian National Guard or the ROTC program at the University of Hawaii, and mainland volunteers, who were imprisoned in the WRA Relocation camps.

After the indignities of being imprisoned and reclassified as enemy aliens, the majority of Nisei on the mainland were angry that their government was now asking them to leave their families in prison camps to fight for liberties that they had lost. They wanted their families to be free and restored to their homes and businesses before they marched off to war. The notion that the Nisei were welcome to volunteer to get shot at was a bitter pill.

During this time of turmoil in the camps, many newspapers added salt to the Nikkei's wounds. Editorials in many cities called for the Nikkei to be sent back to Japan or traded for prisoners of war held by the Japanese government.

Joining the army was so unpopular in 1943 that neighbors frequently ostracized families of those who did volunteer. One father recalled that he did not go to the mess hall, after his son volunteered because neighbors tormented him.

Only one diary entry in the next days mentions anything about the army or the anger over the questionnaire. In spite of the events going on around him, Stan writes about two personal events as memorable.

Jan. 31, Sun., 1943

Today two memorable events occurred. First Freddies [his cousin] *first daughter was born. Also Sach finally finished my sweater. She has been working on it off and on for the last five months. It sure is warm.*

I wrote a letter to Thomas Barry and did my homework.

Feb 1, 1943

Went to Jimmy Yada's house today to go over our chem-

istry. There were three of us altogether. Jimmy, James Nakada and I. We got quite a bit done, even some history.

Seems as if everybody is talking about the new statement Stimson [Secretary of War] gave, which opens enlistment of Nisei into the army again. Jimmie's brother is going to join up.

February 3, 1943

Got an "F" on an Spanish vocabulary test today. Doggone it I better do better on the test tomorrow.

Got an "A" 96% and James got 100% on a test which only 14 people in our history class passed.

February 4, 1943

Doggone it! missed a question on my chemistry test. Oh, well 95% isn't too bad. Took a Spanish test today. Hope I got a better grade than yesterday.

Gee, but the kids at this school are smart! Guys like Paul, Hiroshi, & Jimmy who get all "A's." Can't hardly compete against them.

February 6, 1943

Yesterday I went to Frankie Nishioka's house and met a friend of theirs named Lincoln Kanai. He had been in prison or something until now, because he refused to evacuate. I didn't want to go to Frankie's house, because everytime I go their they feed me & food costs money. But anyway Frankie forced me there. Me & Frankie messed around with his chemical set and I was glad that they didn't feed me anything. But as it neared time to go home & eat they tried to persuade me to eat at their place and I had to refuse because, gee whiz they always feed me like a king or somethin', and so I was leaving then Frankie's mother brought me something wrapped up in a bag, I didn't want to take it but they made me—there was broiled chicken in it I felt like a rat for being so rude as to leave when the insisted so that I stay, but when they gave it to me to take home to eat I felt more like a rat. If I knew I'd have to eat it in the end, I would not have been so rude as to go home, but would have stayed and ate there. Oh well, from now on I guess I had better not go to his house, I don't like to be treated so good. It puts too much of an obligation on me.

Frankie lent me a copy of "Good Earth" by Pearl S. Buck which I started last night and finished this morning. Pretty good book. Most Frank book I have read yet.

Tonite our camp's best basketballers went to Lovell to play them. It's the first "outside" game we have had.

What did Stan mean by "Frank"? *The Good Earth* was one of the few books of the time to treat Asians in a sympathetic and realistic way rather than as "heathen devils" or "inscrutable foreigners." Stan also could have been acknowledging that *The Good Earth* was considered a racy book in 1943 by teenagers, who had limited or no access to explicit sexual literature. "Frank" may have been code for sexy. By today's standards, *The Good Earth* would raise no eyebrows.

An editorial in the Heart Mountain Sentinel on the same day as Stan's Feb. 6th entry claims that the game in Lovell was significant because it was the first friendly invitation from a town in Wyoming. Not all towns accepted the idea of teams from the "Jap camp," as they called it, coming to their towns. Lovell was about 35-40 miles away from Heart Mountain on a narrow two-lane blacktop road. On these trips out into the world, the players were usually unable to stop for a meal or after-the-game snack. Signs in many of the towns made it clear that they were not welcome.

Given the unrest over the so-called loyalty questionnaire, the pressure to volunteer, and the attitudes outside, it is odd that Stanley writes almost nothing about the simmering tensions. On the same day that the editorial appeared about friendships between camps and towns, a decidedly nasty letter was published side-by-side that reveals the deep-seated hatred of many of their neighbors. A letter signed from a "Real American Mother" says in part, "let me ask you this question . . .who started this conflict? Have you thought about that? It wasn't Americans . . . frankly I can't feel you or any of your kind are 100% Americans, I feel the same way as my son . . . once a jap, always a jap. You voluntarily came over here we didn't send for you, you came because you coveted our great country and especially our California, so be satisfied now and take your medicine. Your military power has brought this on you little monkeys . . .I am a 100% American Mother with three precious sons in the service to save our American way of life."

While Stan seems to ignore the unrest, WRA interviews with teachers, written in 1943, indicate that in the upper grades of the high school, the issue of signing the loyalty registration was "argued in our classrooms for several weeks ... some of the youngsters openly claimed in a bold manner that even though they were old enough they would refuse to do so."

In mid-February Stanley did write more fully about one of the tumultuous events he witnessed.

Feb. 12, 1943

Last Tuesday night I went to a meeting held by the army concerning the new order opening voluntary enlistment in the army. There were four men from the army altogether. A lieutenant, two sargents & an Japanese American sargent. They gave a lot of talks telling us how we would benefit if we volunteered. And answered a lot of questions. Said that the reason why they wanted to put us in a separate combat unit was for publicity. A lot of people wanted to know if they could have some guarantees so that after the war was over, they wouldn't have their citizenship taken away, & the lands they own taken. They answered that we would be protected by the 14th amendment in the constitution. Then one man says "well the 14th also is supposed to have kept us out if camp, what about that? The army men answered by saying that 'In time of war the 14th and such do not hold & the army has control & can do practically anything.' Then one man says "what the heck, are we going to get kicked out every time a war comes up." Then the army man said that he agrees that a great injustice was done us when we were kicked out, but he says that the army has realized that what they did was probably wrong, and is now trying to help us to make up for it. He says that if we volunteer it'l do a lot to show our loyalty, and improve the relations & opinions of the American people toward us. It'l show that we are truly Americans, because we volunteered despite the kicking around that we got. On the other hand however he says if we all do not volunteered it'l be the other way around. Instead of improving our relations with the other Americans it would make it worse.

On Wednesday & on Thursday our block's young men got together to discuss it. The niseis wanted to join provided that they got certain guarantees: such as citizenship, land owning & such. However the kibeis opposed this, they said, 'why bother? we want to go back to Japan after the war anyway.' Well all they did was argue & no solution was found for a united action, because the niseis brought up with American ideals just naturally opposed the

*kibeis brought up with Japanese ideals & each thought the other dumb &
grew more hate between themselves.*

The choices over volunteering were not so neatly divided between the Nisei
and Kibei as Stan's diary entry suggests. The vast majority of people inside the
camps in 1943 were opposed to volunteering. Many Nisei felt the call for volunteers brought with it racist insults. Those who wanted to pilot planes or join the
Navy were told that was not possible. They were not welcome in the Air Corps or
Marines; not even the normal ranks of the army. In other words, they were to be
segregated while volunteering to make the ultimate sacrifice—to die for their
country.

Many Issei, as well as their Nisei and Kibei sons, were angered by the government's expectation that after being treated like criminals and stripped of their
freedom that they were expected to serve at all. Others were also angry with the
leader of the JACL (Japanese American Citizens League), Mike Masaoka who pro-
moted the idea that by serving in "suicide squads" the Nisei would prove their loyalty to the United States. In fact, Masaoka was the first to volunteer, but not many
other Nisei did. In Washington, Dillon Myer, the director of the War Relocation
Authority, had predicted there would be as many as 2000 volunteers in Heart
Mountain, but only 38 men volunteered, and half of them failed their physicals.

The government's volunteer program was a gigantic failure. From all ten
WRA camps only about 805 men signed on. Although the army boasted that
more than 3,000 Nisei had volunteered, in truth the greatest number were
American born Nisei from Hawaii, who with few exceptions, were not incarcerated. The Nikkei were such a large part of the Hawaiian population there was no
possibility of imprisoning them all. In fact they were a vital part of the defense
of the islands. It was largely this group of Hawaiian Nisei soldiers who would
soon make headlines as they fought heroically in Europe.

Feb. 19, 1943

*Phew! What a relief! I finally finished my semester tests. I think I did
worse this time than I ever did before. Oh well, I'll find out next week when
my report card comes.*

Feb. 24, 1943 Wednesday

Well today I got my semester grades. Considering the competition here I didn't do so bad.

English	*A*
History	*A*
Algebra	*B*
Chemistry	*A*
Spanish	*B*

Today I got my second Aztec [the school newspaper from his old school, Mark Keppel High School in Alhambra, California] which the school is sending me free. In it was a quote from my letter to them. I said, "Heart Mt. Wyo. is a far cry indeed from balmy Southern Calif. (or is it raining again)" Also "Your loyal Keppel [nickname for their school] supporter and hater of Moors [their rivals from Alhambra High]"

Feb. 27, 1943

Doggone it! I didn't do practically any homework today. Just loafed around and went to the library.

You know theres a thing about this place thats unique and I kinda like and don't like. Its one of the most democratic places I've ever lived in and yet it isn't. What I mean is, though we had our liberty & such, which are supposed to go with democracy, taken away we still live a very democratic life inside. We hold election of officers, & hold block meetings to voice our opinions and most important of all we behold everyone as equals. The rich and the poor were forced into being neighbors & like it. And likewise the good & the bad, the smart & the dumb.

Every one shares the same showers, the same laundry room, & eats at the same mess hall as everyone else. And thats the thing I like, here people respect & like [one] another, not because of their money, of their house, or of cars, but by the only way & the natural way—man for man—their character.

P.S. I registered today. A statement to the U.S. gov't by an American Citizen of Jap. descent.

"Registration day—anxious boys form line to right"

While Stan seems to be trying to convince himself that he has not lost all touch with life in a democracy, he finishes this entry by saying that he signed the questionnaire, rather matter-of-factly. His brother Frank remembers it differently. Frank wrote . . .

The WRA questionnaire that asked, among other questions, 'Will you forswear any form of allegiance or obedience to the Japanese emperor?' How could a loyal American citizen who had never sworn allegiance to a foreign ruler answer this question? If you answered "yes", it was an admission that you had sworn allegiance to the Emperor. If you answered 'no' you were a traitor. This question was similar to "Have you stopped beating your wife?" I submitted a qualified answer that my loyalty was to the United States and never to a foreign power.

Stanley answered question 27, "Yes, if drafted."

Eventually close to 75,000 of the 78,000 Nikkei answered the registration questionnaire. More than 65,000 answered "Yes-Yes" to both questions and were listed as loyal. From all ten camps, a total of 6,733 people answered "No-No" to both questions, and asked for repatriation or expatriation. They were soon segregated with other so-called "disloyals" at Tule Lake, a camp in Northeastern California, until they could be sent back to Japan. Among them were children who had no voice in the decision.

Although many answered yes to both questions, the WRA received and accepted many "qualified" answers like Frank's who objected to the question and explained the reason for not answering yes outright. Frank and others like him were not sent to Tule Lake. They were still considered loyal citizens.

Perhaps the unrest over the loyalty questions and the army stirred up a Stan's longing for home. Leaving camp was not possible for most young Nisei, but in his next entry Stan's writing gave him a way to escape . . .

February 28, 1943

Lonesome for Home
"Gosh but its cold here today! Look Walt, just look at that blizzard out-

side!" I exclaimed as I stood peering out of the window at the snow, flying past our one room apartment.

Walt came over and took a glance and said "Yeah, guess I won't be able to go skating today" and walked back, thinking no more about it as he began to practice his guitar.

I glanced across the room at ma, who was working intently at her embroidery, and who was muttering something about California never having snow.

I peered thru the window again and said to myself "Yeah . . . it never snowed back home . . . .I wish I were home again . . . .I focused my eyes on the snow once more and saw that it was being whipped around more violently by the wind—it was going around in swirls and swirls . . . .and soon my eyes were no longer on it, but look-

ing through it and my mind was far away and was carrying me back one year—back to California! San Gabriel, California!

There I am now! lying in bed and looking out at the tall beautiful eucalyptus yawning in the morning sun as if they too were just awakening. The birds are singing and chirping merrily as they dart into its branches to feed their young. For a while I just stretch and yawn contentedly—then I notice the time opps! its almost nine and here I am still in bed! Oh! Oh! Pop's going to get me if I don't hurry out.

I jump into my clothes, gulp down my breakfast and run out the back door, out into the pleasantly warm and exhilarating spring air.

I know that just so I show my dad I'm awake and been awake for some time, all will be O.K. So I cleverly circle our nursery come from the front and nonchalantly walk past my dad who is watering the plants saying hello Pa! "Kire no he desu-ne!" meaning "beautiful day isn't it!" and my dad smiles back and agrees, and I keep walking by guiltily, not knowing if he guesses what I did or not.

After confirming my "awakening" to my dad and after doing a few chores I go back yard and to inspect this new day of my life, this gorgeous and lively day.

The fresh cool morning air is still warm enough to be comfortable. I look at Papa's young tender plants and see that they have peeped up just a little bit more during the night and the tiny dewdrops on their dark green l leaflets look like diamonds—each sparkling with sunshine.

One of Stan's hobbies was insect collecting.

Big, beautiful, graceful "swallowtails", "monarchs", and "morning cloaks" come flittering by in aimless directions. A morning cloak stops on a flower near me to suck out the sweet nectar—What a "splendidiforous" creature! As the sun shines on the dull black of its wings, it seems to turn into a dark velvety maroon color and the bright yellow fringe of its wings make a pleasant contrast.

But butterflies are not the only ones in the insect world as the fearless, swift morning keen sighted eagles of this miniature world the dragonflies comes darting by me with a powerful droning sound. It darts here and there, then stationary for a time, an away again after some less swift unlucky insect. Then theres the busy bees, industrially collecting nectar from the Orange blossoms & other flowers, at the same time doing their duty in this world—that of fertilizing the flowers.

Gardening was another of Stan's hobbies.

Then I look at the ground, the freshly plowed, soft, warm ground. The soil is fertile and slightly moist, the kind I used to love to poke my bare feet through and wiggle my toes in.

As I bend down nearer I notice the mirads of industrious ants going about their daily toil and remember how I would tear up their homes for their biting me—sweet revenge—but now all is forgotten as I examine them and compare them to how close they resemble our own governments.

As I continue my walk I see the large flaming scarlet and deep yellow or pink blooms of the Hibiscus, the varied colored blooms of human like faces, the pansy and many other flowers and their dark green healthy leaves-all in our own nursery-giving me sort of a feeling of pride.

And there's Marcos, our Mexican hired man, with his shirt off and his bronze back glistening with sweat and sun, working, shoveling dirt on a screen & mixing the soil into the right proportions.

Then I return back to the front of our nursery and see my mom wearing shabby clothes, and patiently transplanting, hundreds of tiny plants into flats. And seeing everyone working hard, and feeling ashamed of myself for loafing around I begin puttering around here and there doing odds and ends and waiting on customers.

And thus it is until night, with cus-tomers coming fast & thick or thick & fast. In the afternoon it is the busiest, and I must carry this & that wait on him or her . . .do this or that. Finally at night I drag myself in at last, exhausted & dirty and see what my sister has prepared——and that reminds me, I thought, I heard the mess hall bell ring!

By early March it was clear, the government's campaign for volunteers had failed. Deeply disappointed and angry, Guy Robertson, the WRA director of Heart Mountain, tried to scare the Nikkei with a threatening memorandum he sent to the block chairmen and managers:

ON VOLUNTEERS . . . (March 5. 1943) TO PEOPLE OF HEART MOUNTAIN:

I feel that it is my duty to point out a number of facts which have either been overlooked or intentionally disregarded by the leaders of Heart Mountain . . .

I would like to ask if the parents realize that a life-long stigma may be borne by their children who fail to recognize and live up to their responsibility in the democratic government and this may reflect upon your oft-mentioned desire to continue to live as good citizens.

The administration has made every effort to help both the Issei and Nisei to . . .show them the effect that their cooperation and non-cooperation will have on the whole future of American-Japanese people who wish to make their future home in America. No pains have been spared to get this problem thoroughly before the people in its full significance . . .

Your government has asked outright that you express your loyalty. They have asked the alien to indicate his friendship . . .Question 28 . . .gives everyone an opportunity to make a definite statement regarding his loyalty or friendship. Your government has offered the citizen an opportunity to volunteer in the armed forces of the United States. They have asked point blank if whether or not you are willing to serve in the armed forces of the United States, to uphold the principle of democracy and freedom to which this country is committed.

The response to these sentiments at Heart Mountain has been very, very disappointing. May I ask the citizen group how they expect to approach their government in asking concessions, whether it is restitution, reparation, or whatever you may ask, when you have more or less repudiated your government by failing to indicate a fair average of enlistment comparable to other relocation centers . . . I would like to point out that you cannot bargain with your government. They are offering you an opportunity. The way you handle the opportunity is, of course, your own business.

In view of the fact that you have not offered your wholehearted support to your government's program, you will be judged by the answer you have made and the attitude expresses. If you have reacted favorable, you will be considered favorably. If you have reacted unfavorably, you will, in all probability, have unfavorable consideration. Surely you understand that you cannot hope to force any issue with the government of the United States.

Guy Robertson, Project Director

To Dillon Myer, Director of the WRA in Washington, D.C., Guy Robertson wrote on March 6, 1943 . . .

Our registration is practically complete at Heart Mountain and in many ways it has been very discouraging. To date we have had 36 voluntary enlistments. In addition . . .we have had 286 citizens ask for repatriation since the enlistment started. We had approximately 12 citizens who had not registered last night.

For the past 30 days I have been trying, through the group leaders in the camp to work up an enthusiastic response to the combat unit. I have felt, and I still feel, that there has been an undercurrent of resistance. We have looked for it every place we suspected it might be found and have never been able to uncover any definite evidence that any individual has been obstruction the program. However the results speak pretty plainly. I met with several groups yesterday but could not get any enthusiastic support in any program to try to increase the number of volunteers.

Stanley writes next to nothing about all these events. Oddly enough, Stan's pages numbered 55 and 56, that would fit here, are missing from the original diary. A sequence of drawings fits in between the entries, but the numbered pages 55 and 56 are marked as missing on the original document. Perhaps Stanley wrote more about his thoughts here and then removed them. Strong feelings were surely in the air and Stanley must have had opinions about these events.

By now Stan has settled into the routines of camp life and making the grade in school continues as his central concern. Despite his silence, the questionnaire and call for volunteers created divisions inside the Nikkei community and its relationship with the WRA and the government.

March 8, 1943   Monday Morning

Friday I started to read Van Loon's Geography and I read it all day Saturday, but now I don't feel like reading it. I'd read it all only I don't have time.

Sunday afternoon I spent ordering my suit from Sears & Roebucks. It cost

Looking westward from the camp to the towering and distinctive shape of Heart Mountain.

about $17.00 but Sach gave me two bucks so that I wouldn't have to pay so much (nice of her wasn't it! She also bought me a lamp about two months ago.) She gave it to me but I think that I'd better pay her back. I don't want people to think that I'm a moocher, besides Sach can use that 2 bucks too. I also bot a shirt and a tie making the total amount which I spent $20.10.

I had to scrimp & save for the last couple of months (since Jan. 15) to buy it. The thing I'm worry about now is whether it will fit in my buget or not. I've got to be thrifty & careful & work out my buget just right, because this buget idea was my own, & pa will laugh his head off if I have to come to him for some money. Heres my allowance, with it I have to buy all my clothes, candy, etc.

Clothing allowance per month		3.75
Pa gives me per month		.25
	total	$4.00

Total clothing allowance per yr.	$45.00
"Pa gives me per yr.	$3.00
total	$48.00

Back home I got about a hundred dollars a year, which I used for anything I wanted. Pa bot me all my clothes, paper & pencils. I started my buget with $16.67- gained $8.27 plus $2.00 making it $10.27. Yesterday I spent $20.10 leaving me $5.54. But if I give Sach back her $2.00 that will leave me only $3.54. I forgot to mention it above but I also spent $.05 in Jan. and $1.25 in Feb.

The main reason why I wanted to start this buget to save money for Pa, and make me feel more independent.

In the summer I'm going to get me a job and make me some extra money.

My one-buck watch

My lamp which Sach bot me

March 15, 1943

Groan! I had a chemistry test today and did I bungle it! The thing is I made my mistakes in mathmatics & not in the actual chem. itself. When I get my paper back tomorrow I'll find out. I think its the worst paper yet.

I wish I knew of a way to improve my mathmatics—it affects my algebra & chemistry. I'm always so darn careless. Think I'll ask my teachers how to be more careful.

March 21, 1943

I got my paper back last week got a "C" doggone it. I've gotta get 100% from now or else!

I spent yesterday, Saturday, studying, playing basketball and buying my suit. My suit I bot with my own money cost me $18.00.

Sunday, today I went to Sunday school, studied my lessons and played basketball. Well that's all for now.

March 29, 1943

Gee I sure haven't been writing in here often. I've been busy as a bee studying my head off so I could bring up my chemistry grade. Last week I got a

perfect 100% in chemistry test so it shows that if I really study I can get really good grades. If I get another 100% on this week's test I've got a chance for an A. That first test in which I got a C did a good job in lowering my grade.

Today I got my history paper back got a 99%. I'm also having a history, English, Spanish & maybe algebra test this week.

Played a little basketball.

April 3, 1943

Yesterday I took three tests, all were tough!

Spent today painting a picture of someone working near our garage back home with Sach's car in the Background.

April 7, 1943

Yesterday I got my report card again. Its about the worst I've ever gotten . . . three B's & one A, and one more grade yet to come. It looks bad but I think I did better than ever my B's were very high & almost A's. If I work hard on all of them I think that I might still manage to get all A's.

April 12, 1943

Today James Nakada got his release to go to Chicago. Gee its going to be sad without him here. He and I had four periods together. He's going all by himself and he's only 16, too. He is going to get a job as a houseboy or something. He will leave on Thursday.

April 14, 1943

Got 100% in Chem. test & history test. Bot James a tie for his going away *present. Boy I'm lucky James is lending me his history book until I finish History.*

April 23, 1943

Today I helped clean the school grounds. In the afternoon went to see Heart Mt. Play Lovell. Our first game with the outside. We beat them 18-5. Baseball.

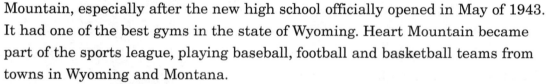

In spite of gas and tire shortages, teams from miles around liked coming to Heart Mountain, especially after the new high school officially opened in May of 1943. It had one of the best gyms in the state of Wyoming. Heart Mountain became part of the sports league, playing baseball, football and basketball teams from towns in Wyoming and Montana.

Both girls' and boys' teams competed within the school and with visitors. Sports were a favorite pastime for adults as well as students who came to cheer for their teams. Although the Heart Mountain players lacked the height to compete well in basketball, they did surprisingly well against the much larger football and baseball athletes.

April 25, 1943 Easter Sunday

Woke up at 4:55 A.M. and went to the sunrise service. It was very cold but was very beautiful—the service as well as the scenery—birds were singing, too.

Came home shivering & jumped back into bed until breakfast, which consists of two sunups, [fried eggs sunny side up] cocoa, and two rolls.

Then went to Sunday School with Walt, Tomo, Hiroshe, George,and Jimmie Yada. We

stayed past Sunday school and thru the Youth Church Service, Saw Corol Anne Shigeko get baptized.

Came home and did a little homework until lunch. After lunch Walt and I went to Frankie Nishioka's birthday party. Did we eat a lot! Chicken, pop, and sandwiches! Came home again and tried to do a little more homework until supper.

After supper I got dressed up again and went to church again with Jimmie Yada and got baptized—So I am now a real Christian. I hope I can live up to that name. Jimmie Yada, Miyuki Yabe, Joe Jason Nishima and a whole lot of others got baptized at the same time with me.

Well that's about all—everyone wants me to turn off the light and go to sleep—so goodnight.

Stanley Hayami

In late April of 1943, anti-Japanese sentiments rose to a new level of hatred when President Roosevelt shocked the nation with news of savage executions of American airmen, captured by the Japanese. They were put to death, in ruthless defiance of international law; prisoners of war were not supposed to be executed. Stanley followed the news with disgust. In his diary he wrote . . ..

April 29, 1943

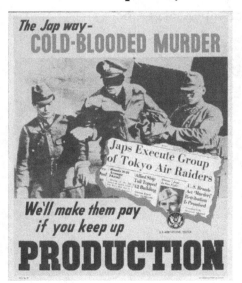

It seems that since the "murder" of the Tokio bombers, who were captured by the Japanese, became known to the public sometime last week, public feeling seems to be pretty strong against us. Doggone it! Every time the Japs over there do something bad, we over here (we who have nothing to do with them over there—and who don't like them any more than anyone else) get it in the neck. Phooey!!

By the time President Roosevelt made the announcement of the executions that April, almost a year had passed since the missing airmen had flown away on a special mission with their leader Lt. Col. Jimmy Doolittle. Plans for their secret mission had been made soon after the Pearl Harbor. The objective was to strike the Japanese mainland, hitting industrial cities and their main target, Tokyo! It shocked the Japanese people that American planes could have come so close to bombing their sacred Emperor!

Lt. Col. Jimmy Doolittle piloted the lead plane of 16 B-25 bombers at 8:24 a.m. on April 18, 1942. Although the attack did not cause as much destruction as future missions would, Doolittle's Raiders gave the United States forces and those on the homefront a tremendous lift in morale. It was just four months after Pearl Harbor and a bitter string of American losses in the Pacific. At the time, Doolittle was celebrated as a great hero. Most of the crews returned, but eight men were captured and three of those captured were executed in October of 1942.

Articles in the Denver Post reflect the anger Stanley refers to in his diary. A front-page story is headlined, "Japanese Threaten To Repeat Atrocity" quoting an enemy broadcaster who says 'Every flyer that comes to Tokyo Has Special Pass to Hell.'

A cartoon in the Denver Post captioned, "Good News From Home" showed a family inside an "Alien Enemy Internment Camp" celebrating. The father is holding up a newspaper with headlines about the execution and the family is smiling happily with exaggerated grins revealing huge stereotypical buckteeth.

In a speech on the Senate floor, Senator Tom Stewart, demanded that the citizenship of Japanese Americans be rescinded and that it was unsound to give the children of Japanese immigrants citizenship. Stewart said . . .

Good News From Home.

"Good News from Home" was the snide caption on this anti-Nikkei cartoon with ugly stereotypical images. Attacks on the Nikkeis' loyalty did not stop, even after they were imprisoned.

They cannot and never can be honest . . . their religion, government and social understanding are opposed to ours. They cannot be assimilated . . . There is not a single Japanese in this country who would not stab you in the back. Show me a Jap and I'll show you a person who is inherently deceptive.

Other stories that week illustrate the wish for vengeance that was sweeping thorough the nation. The chairman of the women's auxiliary of the American Legion said, "Let us at long last realize what the Japanese are. We have leaned over backward to care for the Japs who were sent to relocation camps. We might just as well realize now that they are not and never will be Americans."

In April of 1943, Elmer Davis, Director of the Office of War Information (OWI) attempted to calm public outrage with a radio broadcast, assuring the nation that "There can be no peace with murderers. We must and will gain unconditional surrender." He also told the nation that Americans of Japanese ancestry were outraged by the atrocities. He also issued this press release . . .

> At Camp Shelby, in Mississippi there are three thousand American soldiers of Japanese ancestry; and they turned out yesterday and put the better part of a month's' pay into war bonds to show what they thought of this performance in Tokyo. Thousands of other Americans of Japanese blood, from Hawaii and relocation camps in the west, are now being inducted into the army—all of them tested and known for their loyalty to their country, and all of them just as eager to avenge this sort of behavior as are any other Americans.
>
> *Press release Office of War Information, April 23, 1943*

As upset as Stanley was about the world news, he also noted some bad personal news in the same entry. Perhaps, compared to the bigger news these two items seemed like trifles, hardly worth worrying over.

April 29, 1943

Today I got an F in yesterday's English test. I got a little mixed [up]. Played Ping Pong after school over at the Kei Besshos' recreation Hall. Tried to teach Tsuneo Hiyaki how to ride my bike- he didn't steer very good and hit a fire plug. Hurt himself, too. I think though he didn't say so, [he] pushed my bike's forks back a little.

May 1, 1943 Sat.

Wrote a letter to Jimmie Nakada who is now in Chicago. Helped Pa a little on his victory garden.

Played ping pong in the afternoon. Messed around and did a little homework in the evening. Accomplished very little today.

All through the spring the Denver Post waged a relentless attack, charging that the Nikkei in the camps were being coddled and fed better than civilians outside. There were articles and cartoons about hoarding of food and Nikkei feasting while American families were suffering with rationing. The smear tactics were based on misinformation that nevertheless aroused the anger of the public. Senator Albert "Happy" Chandler charged that the Japanese relocation centers were "fomenting hatred." He falsely reported that 5,000 to 19,000 Young Nipponese expressed their loyalty to the Emperor Hirohito. This was totally untrue. At the same time he charged that the cost of their food was more than 70 million dollars. Another falsehood.

In fact, the food budget per person in the WRA camps was approximately 45 cents per person a day. Forgotten was the fact that a third of the food was grown by the Nikkei in the camps, bringing the average cost per person to 31 cents! This was far less than the average cost of feeding those in state institutions and less than the average 50-60 cents a day spent on feeding soldiers. Those imprisoned in Heart Mountain and other WRA camps had two meatless days a week and a diet heavily based on starches.

Rumors spread that the Nikkei had indoor plumbing. Most Caucasian neighbors had outhouses with no plumbing. It was true the camp's latrines had flush toilets, but they were not in the barracks. The Nikkei had to go out in the freezing cold to use the "indoor" plumbing.

Stan clipped an article about Eleanor Roosevelt, who visited at Gila, a camp in Arizona, and stated that she saw no signs of coddling or abuse. Stan no doubt liked the headline of the article—"First Lady Says Nisei Should Leave Camps." In other interviews she said that she would not want to live in such circumstances. Stan tucked the clipping with Mrs. Roosevelt's photo in his diary for safekeeping.

First Lady Says Nisei Should Leave Camps

BY TIMOTHY G. TURNER

Mrs. Eleanor Roosevelt was in Los Angeles yesterday, filled with a new interest in her life of many interests—the welfare of the young, native-born, citizen Japanese in relocation camps in the hinterland of the Pacific Coast. She believes the sooner they are taken out of the camps, the better.

The President's wife said she had been getting many letters about conditions in the camps, so she came out to see for herself. Some of the letters have said conditions in the camps were outrageous, something like concentration camps in Nazi Germany; others had written that the Japs were being pampered. The investigation, she says, shows that the truth is somewhere between.

Visits Hospitals

Mrs. Roosevelt came here to visit the Navy hospitals at Long Beach and Corona, which she did yesterday. After that she met the press informally. She took her long strides into the room and shook hands with everybody including photographers and Navy enlisted men.

Then the First Lady sat down and started to chat with everybody. She wore a navy blue suit, a light hat and sturdy tan walking shoes. On a table by her side rested a handbag of tan saddle leather, quite as work-a-day as the shoes. There was no red on her fingernails.

May 8, 1943

This morning I woke up to find the ground all white with snow. Imagine, this late in spring too. Wrote a letter to Sam Ashmun.

In the afternoon, James Yada, Tsuneo Hiyake and I went to see the Girl Scout program.

In the evening we went to see Bud Abbott & Lou Costello in "Hold that Ghost."

For those in WRA camps there were memorable dates that punctuated time. In his next entry, Stan recalled the day they were forced to leave their home in San Gabriel. It was an event that remained indelibly etched in memory.

May 14, 1943   Friday

Today marks the end of one year in camp for me. I shall remember that day that I was evacuated for the rest of my life. I shall remember how I stood on the corner of Garvey & Atlantic with about a thousand others- then the buses came and whisked us off to camp. I shall remember the lump which came into my throat as the bus went down the street, and when some of the people on the sidewalks and Mexican laborers in the field, waved to us.

I shall remember the barbed wire, the armed guards, the towers, the dust, the visitors, the food, the long lines, the typhoid shots, my busboy job, my messenger job, the crowded barracks, the nightly talent shows, the good friends I made, my judo lessons, bed count, and finally the leaving on the train to here.

I shall remember the train ride, the sleepless nights, the deserts, the mountains, the beautiful scenery.

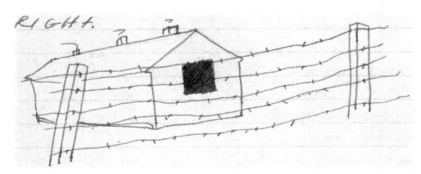

Now that I am here I think of the cold weather I have gone thru, the dust storms, and the rest of my hardships. But I will also remember all the friends I made here, the tough school I went to and I feel no bitterness to the gov't for the evacuation—

though I still feel that it wasn't right.

May 17, 1943

Well just a few more weeks and school will be out. Hooray! Then I can do everything I want to do.

First I want to go to summer school and ~~finnish~~ finish my plane geometry.

Second, I want to attend art classes, and do a lot of neglected art work.

Third, I want to take some more judo lessons where I left off last year at Pomona.

Fourth I want to go to the library frequently, and read a lot of books.

Fifth, I want to work on some writing.

May 22, 1943

"Pues, trabaje en mi composicion en espanol." I worked on it eight hours or more and I still haven't finished it.

Last week . . . I received my report card. I got my best grades so far

English	*A*	*Chemistry*	*A*
History	*A*	*Spanish*	*B (Doggone it!)*
Algebra	*A*		

That's four "A's" and a "B"

About Last week Tunisia and North Africa was finally won after a long battle of approx. six months. Now I guess the allies will go after Europe itself and the final victory over Hitler.

Also last week American forces landed on Attu Island which was held by the Japanese for about a year. I don't know whether we have taken it yet though. If we go get Attu, the next step will be at Kiska, the strongest Nipponese base of the Aleutians.

The Japanese in the meantime have started drives in Burma and China. The Russians and Germans are still pushing each other around in unspectacular defenses and offences. I get bored reading about it so I don't.

The P-47 Thunderbolt has begun to go in action in Europe so I guess I should hear something about it soon. It's supposed to be about the fastest in the present world, the biggest fighter, the longest ranged, the highest ceiling and such. I wonder how it will do against the German Folk-wulf 190.

June 11, 1943

Well today was the finish of one year of hard school work. I got the same grades this semester as for last semester.

English	*A*
History	*A*
Adv. Algebra	*B*
Chemistry	*A*
Spanish II	*B*

WRA-HM-5

Heart Mountain High School
War Relocation Authority, Heart Mountain, Wyoming

Name HAYAMI, STANLEY   Year 1942   Class 11A

GRADE CARD

Subjects	First Semester					Second Semester					Yr.
	6 Wks. Per. 1 2 3			Sem. Ave.	Sem. Crdt.	6 Wks. Per. 1 2 3			Sem. Ave.	Sem. Crdt.	Yrly. Crdt.
Chemistry	B	A	A	A		B	A	A	A	½	1
adv. algebra	A	B	B	B	½	B	A	B	B	½	1
Eng. 11	A	A	A	A		A	A	B	A	½	1
Spanish	B	B	B	B		B	B	A	B	½	1
History 11	A	A	B	A	½	A	A	B	A	½	1

J.K.Corbett
Principal

C.D.Carter
Superintendent

Last semester and during this semester I was never satisfied with the grades I got (3 "A" & 2 "B") because previous to this year and the evacuation I usually got straight "A's". Well now that everything is finally finished and summer vacation has come, I look back over my record and I don't think that it is too bad, considering that about everyone here is so intelligent and studious. Also, the standards were pretty high here. An A was 93% or better. A good thing about all this competition is that it makes me more capable to withstand the time when I go to college.

Gee but there's some really brilliant kids here, especially Paul Mayekawa. Paul sits next to me in History and in front of me in Adv. Algebra. He's a super brain in every subject and has gotten nothing but "A's" all the way through high school. This semester in Chemistry class he didn't miss a single question out [of] about 20 tests which we took, totaling 459 questions. Not even one!! Also last semester he only missed about 4 from 365. He got the highest no. right of all the classes both semesters. Also he got nothing but hundreds in Adv. Algebra and nothing by A+ in History tests. I guess its all the same in the rest of his classes. The only thing that is wrong with him is— he doesn't want to go to college. Isn't that a shame- a brilliant guy like him— he does his work neater than anyone else I know too!

When summer finally rolled around, Stan was lucky enough to get a job at the poster shop. Weeks earlier the *Denver Post* had charged that there were many "painters, drawing what is known as 'professional pay'—the highest in the camp, sit at their easels . . ." WRA officials answered that at the time of the Post reporter's visit there were 13 people employed at the poster shop which cooperates in promoting War Bond and Red Cross drives, fire prevention campaigns, etc. Five of the thirteen were paid $16 a month, eight at $19 a month. Of course, students like Stan were paid less than regular workers. Still, Stan was happy to have a job where he could do what he loved and even get paid!

June 22, 1943

Well, I haven't done much writing in this book for the past week (in fact none) so I guess I'd better do some work to catch up.

First of all, now that it's summer, what am I doing? —In the daytime I work at the poster shop doing odds and ends. Right now I'm helping to make sort of a scrap book to keep souvenir Sentinal papers in. Pretty soon the paper, on which we are going to print (Silk Screen method) a huge navy order for posters, is to arrive. When it comes, I'm going to be plenty busy. When its finished I'm going to be out of a job. I'm asking the commercial artists in there a lot of questions-and thus I'm learning a lot. They say they'll teach me some lettering.

In the way of recreation, what am I doing?— I have begun to take judo lessons again. It's three nights a week (Mon., Wed., Thurs.) In other spare moments I play football. And other few moments I read snatches from the book, We Took to the Woods.

Yesterday Jimmie Yada received a letter from Jimmie Nakada, my best pal which I made in camp, and he let me read it—Jim N. says he really likes it over there (Oak Park, ILL) (By the way, he wants me to accept a job over there.) He goes around with a quiz kid, Jack Lucal, says he's a swell fellow. There's another quiz kid, who lives next door to where he now lives and works. Anyway, from what I gather, he goes to a school, which is abundant in

Stanley experiments with perspective, shadows, and texture.

brains & which is, therefore, very hard.

Well that's about all for now.

June 26, 1943   Sat. Morning

Yesterday my next door neighbor, Ohashi, died. He had been sick for a long time. He left his widow, three daughters, and two sons. His youngest daughter, Emiko, graduated this semester as third highest in the class.

At the poster shop yesterday I had to do a poster—I see where I'm going to have to do a lot of practicing in lettering. The Poster shop is just like school- I learn while I get paid. The commercial artists there are all nice to me and are willing to teach me anything about it. I also have to design a poster.

A couple of days ago, it was Jimmie Yada's birthday (June 24) He is now 17 years. We (Tsnuneo Hiyale, Jimmie, Kei Bessho, and I) gabbed until one o'clock AM.

Thursday I signed up for summer school. I have to finish up my plane geometry. I'm taking it in the afternoon from 2:30–4:30.

Artists created posters for the Navy as well as for inside the camp.

Stan's enthusiasm for summer school probably had a lot to do with the totally modern Heart Mountain High School building that had finally replaced the barracks. It consisted of 40 classrooms, a medical clinic, offices, shops for vocational agriculture, home economics, and a combined gymnasium-auditorium. Adult education classes were held here as well. Students from other towns marveled at the size of the gym—considered by many the best in Wyoming!

Stan makes no mention of the new and improved classrooms and supplies, but he had not complained about the old barrack schools, either. He continues to focus on his grades, which seem to improve in the new setting. The WRA was accused of robbing teachers away from the classrooms of Caucasian students outside the camps by offering higher salaries. Although some were attracted by the chance to earn more, many of the teachers who came to the camps did so in spite of their family or friends' negative opinion. Some signed on because they felt the incarceration was unjust; others had longstanding friendships with Nikkei schoolmates and neighbors. For those fresh out of college, this was the first job some of the teachers ever had.

Many of the newly hired teachers rented rooms in nearby Cody or Powell, but from the start some chose to live in housing inside the camp. They had indoor plumbing, a separate mess hall, and more comforts than the Nikkei. It was hardly an easy life, but those who lived "inside" tended to socialize more and mentor their high school students.

Not all the teachers were Caucasians hired from outside. Some faculty members were Nisei, who like their students, were prisoners. Although many had earned advanced degrees in science, engineering, and other subjects, they were given temporary licenses to teach in the state of Wyoming, with the proviso that they would not be welcome or licensed in Wyoming to teach outside the camp or after the war. Caucasian teachers earned $2000 annually while Nisei teachers were paid $19 dollars a month or $228 annually!

Students needed coats in cold, crowded barrack classrooms during the first school year. High School Geometry Class,1942. Photograph by Hansel Mieth.

Although the new school was a great improvement over the old barracks, for Stanley it could not compare to the new high school he had left behind in California. His older brother and sister had attended Alhambra High. It was an older school and overcrowded. Because of the migration of the Okies during the depression and the growth of farming in the area, there was a serious need for a new school in the San Gabriel area. Shortly before the war, Stanley had been lucky enough to attend the brand new Mark Keppel High. His longing for that lost place is never far from his memory.

Out of the blue, Stanley seems to have assigned himself an essay expressing his feelings about the evacuation. Since teachers were encouraged not to discuss these events with students, it is likely that Stan just needed to put his

A new modern Heart Mountain High School was opened in 1943.

thoughts on paper about this major event. There is no date on this page, but it follows the June 26th entry.

MY VIEWPOINT ON THE EVACUATION

Many people have written of the evacuation-have debates about it in heated discussions—and have wondered how we feel.

Well since I am one of those evacuated, although I may not be typical, but then who is? I will try to set down in writing—what I think about it?

First of all, do I think that is was constitutional? No. I do not. We did not go thru the due processes of law. They didn't have any evidence. (it has been proven that there has been no sabotage done by the Japanese in Hawaii or the West Coast prior to or after the evacuation) However, it could have been legal, since the military doesn't have to go by the constitution in time of war.

Do I think racial prejudice was involved? Yes I do. If it were not, how does one account for the fact that German and Italian aliens were not evacuated while Jap. American citizens as well as Japanese aliens were evacuated. Don't tell me we were the more dangerous. Germans and Italians can get closer to defense plants than a Japanese can.

Do I think that it was worthwhile from the standpoint of the gov't. This is a very tough question as I don't think know all the facts and what I say would be my opinion alone. My answer is that I don't believe that it was worthwhile to the gov't. Out of the 115,000 Japanese evacuated I doubt if there were any really dangerous ones. Instead of evacuating all of us - they should have kept an eye on us and just evacuated the worst of us. The evacuation also cost the gov't a tremendous amount of money and is continuing to do so. California faced a serious labor and food shortage due to the evacuation. Also many Nisei lost faith in America.

Do I think the evacuation did or will do some good? Yes—-for one thing it broke up the heavy concentration of Japanese on the Pacific coast, and eventually all of them will be spread out over the whole U.S. without looking conspicuous. However, once we start forming those cliques (such as Little Tokio) and start isolating ourselves people will begin to misunderstand us, grow suspicious of us, and prejudices will form against us again.

Well now that I have gone over the whole Goddam situation what do I think in the final analysis.

I think the whole mess was unnecessary and a lot of trouble could have been avoided. However it did some good-that of breaking up the cliques. I personally will proceed to forget the whole mess, will try to become a greater man from having gone thru such experiences, keep my faith in America, and look forward to relocation and the future.

"Don't be afraid of opposition. Remember a kite rises against, not with the wind"

Hamilton W. Mabie

June 27, 1943   Sun.

I don't tell this to anyone because they'll figure that I'm a queer (Maybe I am.) Every once in a while I feel tremendously moody—When I get that way I sort a want to get away from the people who are continually around me (in camp there are people wherever you go) to a quiet place outside, where the fresh air blows, where only nature lives, where no one can bother me, and where I can contemplate and think as deep as I want. And that is the trouble with camp—there is practically no such place. One can't do things like that here, people will bother you, think you're stuck-up if you ignore them, or think you're absent-minded. (I really do get absent-minded too.) And thats one reason I don't like George Azuma so much—when I'm sitting, reading or thinking he'll push me over or do something to me and then try to shake me out of it. I guess his intentions are good and playful but it sure burns me up. And because it does it burns me up more to be mad just because someone tries to disturb my concentration. I can't very well explain to him- its too silly for someone as young as me to say that I'm trying to do some deep thinking. I'm just worrying about what will happen if someday I lose my temper (I rarely do) when he does that- I may do something drastic.

And I guess all this is the main reason I like the books Cross Creek *and* We Took To the Woods. *They both describe places where a person may get away from it all, get down to simple life and nature, and do thinking or painting or writing with no one to bother them. The places they live in are places where other people do not govern there their lives but where they can lead their own life.*

Thats the kind of place I want to live in when I grow up.

In the afternoon I took about a fifteen mile ride on my bike. Was I tired. I went to the relocation limits. Went to see a movie in the evening, too.

These last two entries reveal how much Stanley feels the need to express his opinions and feelings. His diary is the solitary, private, and personal place where he can fulfill this need, a place where no one bothers him.

Monday June 28, 1943

Went to work in the morning. Went to summer school (Geometry class) in the afternoon. Will go to Judo tonight.

Sunday 11, 1943—July

Well, another week has gone by; the hot Wyoming sun beat down as usual and the dry stuffy wind from the south shifted the dust around some more.

While on the battlefronts of the world exciting action took place. In the South Pacific MacArthur & the Allies started an offensive to take Rabaul & the control of the Solomons. Today's radio said Munda will probably be captures with the next week. While this was going on the invasion of Europe finally took place. Sometime around Saturday the Allies attacked & landed at Sicily. And have established themselves satisfactorily.

Everything is going along OK. At the poster shop I work there on the Navy order which will be finished soon. During my spare time there I read the book SO YOU'RE GOING TO BE AN ARTIST

After reading it and after listening to Tad, the commercial artist who has done work in New York, I feel like either becoming a commercial artist, industrial designer or architect. If I work at these I will at least be able to make a living, however, my final goal will be the fine arts.

I'm now reading ONE WORLD *by Wendell Willkie and* MEN WHO MAKE THE FUTURE.

Thursday 22, 1943 [July]

Finished reading One World *by Wendell Willkie. Very good. The chapter I like best is chapter 13 "Our Imperialism at Home". He discusses racial prejudice, minority groups & such in that chapter.*

Sunday 25, 1943 [July]

Stanley's drawing looks like a study for Tempo (see pg. 110).

Benito Mussolini Quit as Premier (Dictator) of Italy today.

Sunday August 1, 1943

Last Thursday Frank left for New York. When he shook my hand to say good-bye, I could hardly say anything because of the lump in my throat. Gosh its queer. I argue and quarrel with him, but when it comes to where he leaves I feel kinda sad. Shig Iseri and Coya Iwamoto (Frank's good pals) Anson, Eddie, Margaret and Alice and Papa were there too. Ma went to sewing so she wasn't there. Sach said she couldn't stand saying good-bye so she didn't go. Walt was working in the poster shop.

Yesterday a friend of Frank's returned from Billings, Montana and dropped in to give us a big bag of candy, which Frank had bought when he passed thru there, & which he had given to him to bring to us.

Right now, summer school is almost finished & there will be about a month interlude before school starts again, so I feel like going out to do some work & earn some money. Then I'll be able to buy some needed art supplies.

These sad farewells were clearly difficult for all the members of the Hayami family. There was no way of knowing when they might see each other again. Oddly, Sach has hardly been mentioned for months. Here it is August of 1943 and surprisingly, she is still in Heart Mountain. It was November of 1942 when her parents gave her permission to go to school in St. Louis. But getting clearance and making applications all took time. Many young adults went out on part-time work leave and then returned. But those who were going to school were not expected to return.

Their brother Frank had no intention of ever returning. This is how he remembers his first months of freedom . . .

By August 1943, the government had decided that I was no longer considered dangerous to the public safety, and that I could leave camp to any destination in the United States with the exception of the area under the Western Defense Command which included the entire Pacific Coast . . . .Therefore with one suitcase, a railroad ticket and $100 in cash, I took off for New York City to seek my fame and fortune. In those days, I was carrying a 4C draft card (4C meaning "enemy alien") even though I was a native born American. I traveled without too much trouble from authorities or confrontations from white Americans since they all took me for an American Indian or a Hawaiian because of my deep tan.

The only work I could find was in restaurants bussing the dishes off of the tables and slopping them into the garbage cans. My 4C draft card did not help me to get any work in the engineering field since most of that work was of a military nature.

Aug 16, 1943

16 days have gone by since I last wrote, but not much has happened during that time. On the many war fronts the same is true. Munda in the Pacific fell to the Yanks, finally sometime last week. Sicily is about to be taken and Russia has been pushing Hitler back this summer.

I quit my work at the Poster shop on the 2nd of this month and finished my geometry, in which I got an A. I was going to go pick peaches in Colorado, but something went wrong and it was cancelled. Therefore I'm practically loafing now, except for my art class, which I enrolled in just before I finished my geometry.

By the way, now that I've finished my geometry I'm completely caught up in my subjects so I'll go thru a complete record of my work to date..

According to my record I may graduate. I have 29 "A's" and 7 "B's" for a 93% or a rating of 2.8 which is two tenths less than a perfect 3.

Everyone seems to be leaving. Frank and many of Stan's friends have gone or are about to leave. There is no doubt that Stan is feeling left behind and anxious.

Aug. 17, 1943

Last night I didn't have ~~more~~ enough time to finish.

Well Frank got to New York last week or so. He wrote back and told us what a big city New York is. He sounds kinda lonely. People think he's Chinese. He says he will have to work on some other job till his defense clearance comes through.

Kei Bessho who sat in front of me in Chemistry class last year went to Chicago 2 weeks ago. Mits Inouye and Ralph Yanari, also in my chemistry class, and Albert Saijo, who worked in mess hall 5 with me back in Pomona, went together to work in the hospital at the Univ. of Michigan at Ann Arbor. They will try to get into the school later.

Segregation will start soon. 1st 500 from Tule Lake arrive Sept. 13, Sept 14. 1st 400 from our camp leave for Tule Lake. 2000 will get there from Tule Lake altogether.

In all ten WRA camps, those who had refused to sign yes to questions 27 and 28 on the loyalty questionnaire that spring were now being shipped to Tule Lake, in Northern California, where they would be segregated with the others classified as "disloyals." Among those were hundreds who asked to be repatriated to Japan after the war. Many young people who were citizens did not want to go to Tule Lake. But since they were still minors they had to do as their parents said. In fact many of them were forced to go to Japan with their families after the war and found they were not especially welcome.

Those in Tule Lake who had signed "yes-yes" were being sent to other camps, including Heart Mountain. However, there were some families classified as "loyal" who decided against moving yet a third time and remained in Tule Lake.

Although it appears from his diary that Stan was not especially involved in the upset over segregation, the departures were sad events separating families and friends who might not ever meet again. It also brought a new influx of families who arrived to musical welcomes by the boy scouts of Heart Mountain.

For Stan the departure of close friends and yet another part of his family was surely more personally upsetting. His diary now records a string of sad goodbyes.

Goodbye to the strains of "Star-Spangled Banner"

Aug 25, 1943
Cousin Eddie left for the Univ. of Cincinnati today.

August 31, 1943
Sach left for Chicago—It was windy—Sach had some tears in her eyes— though she tried hard to fight them back—don't blame her. James Yada left yesterday for River Forest, ILL.

Sept 13 Monday [1943]

Italy surrendered last week. Looks like the tide has turned to an allied victory. Lord Louis Montbatten in command of all Allied South East Asian Forces. Churchill and Roosevelt had another conference in Quebec. Japanese evacuated Kiska just before American forces landed. Was surprise move. They usually fight to the last man.

Sach is going to American Academy of Arts. She wrote and said she will work for a doctors family while she goes to school.

Frank is in New York still waiting for his defense plant clearances. He's working as a bus boy in a cafeteria while he's waiting. He sent a lot of food last week. A girl, Miwako Oana, who wrote "Scratch Pad" for the Sentinel relocated to New York. She writes and says she saw Frank.

My lifelong friend Sam Gates is now in the Air Corps.

Sept 15, 1943

Got to ration out my time.

Sept 18, 1943

Last nite I went to a farewell party for Schiko Uyeda who is leaving for Tule Lake. I tried dancing for the first time, too.

Wrote a letter today to Grace [Sach], Sammy Gates, and Johnny Saito. What a variety of places, eh? Chicago, air corps— California, Relocations camp—Poston Arizona.

Sept. 21 1943

Today the first trainload from Tule Lake arrived. Also the first trainload from our camp left. Schinichi Ito came over today to talk with me tonight too. He certainly has changed a lot! Back home he was the last person I thought would go to a social, but things have changed . . . he goes to practically every social now. Back home he was always sour faced; but here he is more pleasant faced. He used to talk to me about the kick he got out of doing bad things, but now he tells me about all the fun he has going to dances and such. I guess I haven't changed much though.

Sept. 23, 1943

Tonight after I went to see a movie about Ohio, Paul Mayekawa, Tsuneo Hiyake, and I talked for about an hour outside the auditorium about the many puzzles of our world and our universe. After talking about how big the universe is—so big that we couldn't imagine how big it is, one of us remarked how silly it is that the people of our little earth are making such a big fuss and rumpus over it.

Heart Mountain's basketball team played against schools from Wyoming and Montana.

~~Sept.~~ Oct. 1, 1943

Well today our high school beat the supposedly strongest team in the Big Horn Basin—Worland. It was our first game and we beat them 7–0. The radio gave reports today that Japanese troops are fighting in Italy now—Japanese American Troops. A German prisoner saw them and was amazed. Hope they do good.

Oct. 31, 1943

Well, many things have happened since I last wrote.

There's still a big fight going down New Guinea way, with MacArthur trying to put a pincers on the Japanese base at Rabaul, Salamaua and Lae were taken long ago.

Over in Italy, the going seems to be tough and slow. The Japanese American troops, there, were reported to be doing very good!

The Russians have crossed the Dneiper River and seem to be doing good. With winter coming the Russians should do even better. In Moscow, the Big Three—U.S., Russia and Britain—represented by Cordell Hull, Stalin, and Anthony Eden, are holding a historical conference.

From England to Germany & back the bombers seem to be busy bombing the life out of Germany. (I feel kind of sorry for the civilians of Germany who are being bombed, but I guess this is war. They were bombing England before and I guess that was war too.)

Today the sky was cloudy and the ground was muddy from yesterday's rain. The wind blew cold blasts from the north. Outside, people walked about *huddled in heavy black peacoats. Inside our room, the big Army coal stove kept things nice, warm and cozy. Papa seems to worry quite a bit about Frank. Frank hasn't written to us for about a month, so I guess I worry a little myself.*

I guess we worry more since we heard about Jimmy M. Jimmy was riding on a bus from Billings to Cheyenne and something happened on that bus that caused his being put in jail as insanely dangerous. According to the police he became crazy so someone slugged him. Mr. M.[his dad] visited him in jail, says he is crazy and won't even wear clothes. He has a lot of head bruises. He (Mr. M.) thinks they hit his head and made him crazy. The question, then, is, was he crazy before or after the man hit him? I've known Jimmy since Pomona. He's a big, happy go lucky, not too smart, boy. At times I've noticed him to be slightly queer in what he says. Mama says his mother's sister's son was batty too. So maybe there's a strain of insanity running in their family. I feel kinda sorry for Mr. M.-he's worried sick. Just last week too, his other son, Frank, was almost killed by a man in Cody, who tried to run him over. Frank wasn't the only one though. There were other boys with him. The man returned later with a rifle, but the [other] man, for whom Frank and his gang were working for, wrestled the gun away from him and knocked him out.

I guess that's why Pop and us guys are kind of worrying about Frank—he should of wrote to us long before.

Sach is having trouble too. She lost her job and had to move elsewhere. However she wrote to us last week.

Lately, I haven't been feeling so hot. About 3 months now.

I have no pep and my feet and arms feel heavy. My nose isn't so good either—I always have to blow it and spit mucus from my mouth. I seem to be awfully nervous at school too—I sweat profusely from under the armpits and hands. Maybe I have T.B. or high blood pressure or bad heart or all; and then maybe it's just my imagination and my not getting enough exercise. I'm also getting thinner than ever and my veins on my arms bulge out. At any rate, I'd better go see the Doc soon. I'll wait until things seem brighter though. Pa and Ma are worrying too much right now without me.

My grades for the first 6 weeks were:

Art	*A*
Solid Geometry	*A*
Physics	*A*
Eng. Lit.	*B*

Nov. 1, 1943

Well, Frank wrote us at last—he's O.K. Says he gets tired easily. Bad. Went with a Chinese to a Chinese Meishi dinner Sunday. Pop (and we) were certainly relieved.

Nov. 9, 1943

Last Friday Nov. 5th was Mama and Papa's Silver Wedding Anniversary. They've been married for 25 years. Sach sent them a salt and pepper set.

Nov. 21

Doggone it, I finally got up enough courage to go to the clinic last Saturday. They told me to come on wk. days. So I went again last Mon.—they were too crowded, so I went to see the school nurse— she hadn't moved into her office yet. So here I am still worrying about my health.

Sach got fired from her 1st job and now has another—Frank asked her to come to New York, 'cuz he could help her then, if she gets into difficulties.

Frank sent us a letter yesterday asking Walt & my chest measurements &

also our shoe number—I wonder what he's up to?

Ojisan and Obasan [uncle and aunt] who are now in Cincinnati sent us some stuff yesterday. Freddy and Buddy went to Denver. Willie has been *transferred to Camp Shelby.*

Nov. 27

It seems as if the whole family has colds at present. Papa has a bad cough. Walt took a day off yesterday in bed. Mama, too, she looks kinda anemic. And my health is bad enough! I guess I'll try going to the doctor's again. Hope they're not busy. Doggone! When the family gets looking like it is, I feel like hell! I feel that I probably got T.B. and am probably passing it on to everyone else.

About a week and a half ago, it dawned on me that maybe coffee was the cause of my feeling nervous, so I stopped drinking it. Incidentally, I used to drink nothing but milk until about two months ago when I started feeling "not so hot" in the stomach. So I stopped the milk and my stomach immediately got better— so I guessed that something was wrong with that milk and switched to coffee.

Well anyhow after the layoff of coffee—(they won't give me milk anymore either) (I drink water) I notice that my extreme nervousness has slightly depreciated and I don't feel quite so tired anymore.

However, I feel that the main trouble with me lies in my not getting enough sunshine or exercise, or because I have contracted some contagious disease. At any rate, I'd better make a determined effort to find out and get better.

Especially, "get better", because Frank sent me and Walt a letter saying that if he (Frank) can get a job in New York he'll try to get me out there with him so I can attend either Columbia (ohh!) or City College. At any rate (if we all keep in good health) we'll probably head for New York sometime next spring. We, meaning the whole family.

Frank seems to be getting along O.K. now in New Jersey. His job isn't so good, but he's thinking of moving on to New York again. He's made a lot of new friends, especially friendly Japanese and half-Japanese girls. Says he goes bowling quite often and also dancing.

Sach wrote us an 11 page letter-all about her new job in Chicago. She's house-girl again, but says its better this time.

One of those half-Japanese girls Frank met was a girl named Martha Okazaki. Her father was an Issei who had immigrated to New York from Japan and her mother was from Northern Ireland, a Protestant. Martha's mother took her to Japanese Language school on Saturdays and her father, who became a

Christian, took her to Sunday school at the Japanese Church in New York.

There were not many Japanese American families in New York in the 1940's but as many Nisei from the camps began to arrive, the WRA threw dances for them so that they would meet each other. Martha remembers going to such dances. In fact, that is where she met Frank Hayami. He had hoped to find work as an electrical engineer, but the best job he could find was as a bus boy in a cafeteria across from the Empire State Building. He worked there for a while until he found an ad for work at a factory where he blew glass tubes for radios. That job was in New Jersey, but he had friends, especially Martha, whom he visited often in New York.

Dec. 1, 1943

I pray that I will never get to feeling too cocky or superior or too low or inferior. At present, whenever I feel too superior, I use as my yardstick someone much better. If I feel inferior I get busy and work to make myself better!! I hereby make one of the axioms or laws of my life.

> *NEVER USE AS YOUR YARDSTICK*
> *PERSONS LOWER THAN YOU—*
> *BUT MEASURE YOURSELF WITH A*
> *YARDSTICK SO MUCH GREATER*
> *THAN YOU—THAT YOU CAN NEVER*
> *GROW TO EQUAL IT*
> *(BUT WILL ALWAYS HOPE YOU CAN.)*

You know, whenever I need refreshment and feel kinda tired of life, or whenever I need comfort, or to reduce a swelling head, or lift my morale—I look at the stars. They also seem to have a silent rhythm like music. I wonder what they think? They were there when I came and they will be there when I leave. To them, my life is microscopial—just a flicker in eternity. I will write more of this later.

Dec. 5, 1943

Man, all I did this week wk. end was to read Anthony Adverse. I've read 702 pages to date. Have about 522 (total length 1224 pgs.) pages to go. Its a pretty good book though so I guess its worth it. Learning a lot too.

Where am I going? I study my head off habitually—

I eat, sleep, and etc. But where is my goal? I still haven't decided what I want to be. What am I going to leave the earth as my contribution? I feel like Anthony when he was young.

Right now I'm probably the most confused ~~man~~ boy alive. I'm mixed up about everything. I have faith in almost nothing.

Dec. 9, 1943

Went to the hospital to give book report to teacher, Miss Sudderth. We talked about books then about many other things. Very interesting talk.

Received some of the things I ordered from Favor Rhul & Co. But most of the things didn't come.

Dec. 16, 1943

Two weeks ago, we got our report cards. I finally got all A's. First time since I evacuated.

Dec. 23, 1943

Today was my birthday. Am 18 now. Guess I'm getting to be an old man. I'm still not in college, though. Tsuneo is also a senior (what a brain too) but he's only 15.

Went ice skating for the first time this season with Tsuneo. Police kicked everyone off though-said it was dangerous because of cracks.

Favor-Ruhl Co. sent me rest of my stuff, finally, except for 42 cent brush which they charged me for and a watercolor set, which they sent me back a check.

I guess I'd better register with the draft board, maybe tomorrow.

Although the Nisei were not yet subject to the draft they did have to register with the Selective Service draft board. At 18, Stan was now old enough to serve, if he volunteered, like some of the graduates from the class of 1943. In fact, Ted Fujioka, the popular student body president was one of the young men who had done exactly that.

Dec. 25, 1943

Well today was Christmas. I had a cold—still do—so I stayed at home all day. Right now they're having a party in our mess hall.

Like last year—I received presents from people I don't even know. This time I got a present from a person named Luther Haines, one from a girl named Betty Ann Flanigan, one from a couple— Mr. & Mrs. F.L. Mulfood and another from a group in West Richmond, Indiana. The presents were a jig saw puzzle, a pair of socks, a handkerchief, and a comb case.

I'm going to write the people as soon as I can. They must be good people to send me something.

Sach sent me a shirt. She also sent Pop and Walt shirts and Mom a blouse. Must have sacrificed a lot.

In the evening Pop and I talked about this and that. Pop told me about Ojisan and how he was (Ojisan) almost a millionaire before the depression.

Of Ojisan going to Japan to try to sell cars and trucks. Pop says that during my life I will have my ups and downs so be ready and careful when you're up so you won't fall so hard when you have your downs.

A Christmas card silkscreened at the poster shop. Artist is unknown. In a few weeks, many would receive another kind of "Greeting."

1944

My heart tells me to be a Artist — writer. My mind tells me to be practical and be someone like an architect.

I'm inclined too follow my heart — not without due reasoning though.

1944

1944 begins for Stanley without any resolutions to keep or break. His biggest worries are still his grades. It is just a few months until graduation and his grades are going to count. His brother Frank, sister Sach, and many friends had already left Heart Mountain or were planning to go soon. Stanley was hoping to do the same—maybe even go to Columbia University and live with Frank in New York City! Stan writes only a few entries before the big news breaks, news that would change everything.

On January 20, 1944 the government announced an explosive piece of news that rocked the camps. Last year's volunteer program for army recruits had failed, but there was a way to correct that. Secretary of War Stimson announced that Japanese Americans were now eligible for the draft. Joining the army was no longer a matter of choice. Any time after your 18th birthday the government could send you a letter of "Greetings!" You were required to report for your physical exam. If you did not do so, you could go to jail.

Jan 7, 1944

Well here it is another year already. Hope it will be much better than last year. I'm sorry I haven't written for such a long time, but I've been so busy writing essays and studying for tests. Last week I took a physics test. I know how to work everything. I had even gone to the trouble of working all the review problems in the back of the book—that's all except one of them. And what happens? That problem happens to be in the test and I missed it. However I managed somehow to work it, and got the answer right except for a decimal pt. on that one problem!

Sach sent me the watercolor set I sent for. She's going to New York this month. Will write more later it's late now about 10:45.

Jan 17, 1944

Right now 9:00 o'clock P.M. We're having a terrific dust storm. The windows are closed, but the dust still gets in. The windows are rattling. I can smell the dust and when I blow my nose it is noticeable on my handkerchief. It's in my teeth and my hair and my desk is covered with it.

Sach is in New York now with Frank.

Jan. 20

Well I ended up with all A's for once. Well not for once, 'cuz I used to get all A's before too. Last year was the worst.

It could be that last year was bad, but the news that had just arrived was even worse! This is the day the big news broke, but surprisingly, Stanley does not write that the army has changed its mind again. He did not write for a few days, perhaps to give himself the time to think through what will happen next. January 24th is one of the few entries where Stan confides his concern. He has not received a draft notice, but a Selective Service registration questionnaire, now that he is 18. Still, signing this form was no longer just a formality. At eighteen, Stanley is now classified as 1-A and is certain to be drafted after graduation.

News of the draft made headlines in the Heart Mountain Sentinel *and the* Eagle, *the school paper.*

January 24, 1944

Well I haven't done any writing in here for such a long time now that I'd have to do a lot of writing [to] say everything and to cover everything about what I am thinking—and I have done a lot of thinking. I read books like Anthony Adverse and the Complete Life of Erskine.

But today I'll just write of more immediate things that are worrying me. Selective Service was just opened up recently to Nisei again. And recently I turned 18, draft age. Well, last week on Thursday or so, I received a question-naire. And being very busy and hard pressed I didn't get around to looking at that thing until tonight. Well, I read the instructions and it said "to be returned by the 25th or you are punishable by fine or imprisonment." Well tomorrow is the 25th!!! And even if I mail it tomorrow it'll never get to

California by about the 29th. So maybe I'll go to jail! I won't mind the jail so much, but it will be mighty humiliating! I've never been in jail before. Maybe they'll excuse me though. Well, anyway I don't care!

News of the draft was received with strong, but mixed emotions. Once again the Nikkei were faced with few choices. While there were those who saw this as a way to prove their loyalty and patriotism, it was impossible to be blind to the injustice of their situation. Stanley, along with all the young Japanese American men of his generation, was an American citizen, imprisoned in a concentration camp, was now expected to leave his family as prisoners while he served his country. His government was demanding that he and all Nisei Sons be willing to lay down their lives to defend a country that had failed to defend their rights.

Stan's diary entry about his fear of being arrested comes just two nights before three hundred Heart Mountaineers met to form the Fair Play Committee (FPC), the group that would challenge the legality of drafting the Nisei. Once again, Stan writes nothing about the furor in the camp over the draft and the almost nightly meetings throughout February and the beginning of March. They were often noisy meetings with long speeches by those who decided that they had been silent too long.

Nor does he mention that one of the leaders of the Fair Play Committee is none other than his cousin Alice's husband, little Polito's father, Paul Nakadate. In fact, Paul is not merely a member of the FPC, he is their Vice Chairman.

United with their motto, "one for all—all for one," the Fair Play Committee issued a series of manifestos declaring their intention to defend their Constitutional rights and the fundamentals of "our democratic institutions." They were willing to serve only if the government recognized their birthrights as citizens and restored them to their former status. To them, the very fundamentals of Democracy were at stake.

On March 4th, 1944 the Fair Play committee issued a bulletin that stated their willingness to defend their country *[see sidebar, next page]*.

In a matter of weeks, while Stan was finishing his senior year, sixty-three young Japanese American men in Heart Mountain who refused to appear for their physicals were indicted by a federal grand jury in Cheyenne, Wyoming. They were charged with resisting the draft. There were so many young men that they had to be put into jails all over the state.

We the members of the FPC are not afraid to go war — we are not afraid to risk our lives for our country. We would gladly sacrifice our lives to protect and uphold the principles and ideals of our country as set forth in the Constitution and the Bill of Rights, for on its inviolability depends the freedom, liberty, justice, and protection of all people including Japanese Americans and all other minority groups. But have we been given such freedom, such liberty, such justice, such protection? NO!! Without any hearings, without due process of law as guaranteed by the Constitution and Bill of Rights, without any charges filed against us, without any evidence of wrongdoing on our part, one hundred and ten thousand innocent people were kicked out of their homes, literally uprooted from where they have lived for the greater part of their life, and herded like dangerous criminals into concentration camps with barbed wire fences and military police guarding it, And then, without rectification on the injustices committed against us nor without restoration of our rights as guaranteed by the Constitution, we are ordered to join the army thru discriminatory procedures into a segregated combat unit! Is that the American way? NO! The FPC believes that unless such actions are opposed now, and steps taken to remedy such injustices and discriminations immediately, the future of all minorities and the future of this democratic nation is in danger.

Thus, the members of the FPC unanimously decided at their last open meeting that until we are restored all our rights, all discriminatory features of the Selective Service abolished, and measures are taken to remedy the past injustices thru Judicial pronouncement or Congressional act, we feel that the present program of drafting us from this concentration camp is unjust, unconstitutional, and against all principles of civilized usage. Therefore, WE MEMBERS OF THE FAIR PLAY COMMITTEE HEREBY REFUSE TO GO TO THE PHYSICAL EXAMINATION OR TO THE INDUCTION IF OR WHEN WE ARE CALLED IN ORDER TO CONTEST THE ISSUE . . . "

Fair Play Committee Bulletin,
March 4, 1944

Their trial was the largest mass trial in the history of Wyoming. Despite the fact that these young men believed they were doing their duty as American citizens to uphold the Constitution, they were all found guilty of draft evasion and violating the Selective Service Act and sentenced to federal prison for two to three years. A few months later the seven leaders of the FPC, including Stan's cousin by marriage, Paul Nakadate, were also tried, found guilty and sent to prison for unlawful conspiracy to counsel, aid, and abet violators of the draft.

This was a time when the young Nisei struggled with making decisions that they should never have needed to face. Had they been treated as citizens, retained their freedom, and been accepted into the service of their choice, none these events would have happened. There would have been no terrible division within the Nikkei community that shadowed the lives of so many families for decades after the war.

All through these stormy times, the camp newspaper, the Heart Mountain Sentinel remained firmly on the side of the WRA and the JACL. The resisters and their families were considered an embarrassment by many; often their families were shunned. In fact, the mother of one of the resisters was so upset, she eventually took her own life. It is somewhat puzzling that Stan writes nothing about these events. Many of the resisters were close to his age.

Yet it is during this same time that stories of the outstanding valor and achievements by the first Nisei troops started to fill the news. For those inside the camps, more attention and pride focused on the heroes of the 442nd Regimental Combat Team and their amazing record.

Like Stanley Hayami, the great majority of Nisei did eventually serve in the newly formed 442nd Regimental Combat Team. Fewer than 400 Nisei resisted the draft and became "prisoners of conscience" in court battles over their constitutional rights as citizens. The resisters ended up in federal prisons defending their beliefs and accepting the consequences. It has taken decades for the Nikkei community to begin to acknowledge that the resisters were not cowards but fighters defending the rights of all Americans. In their own very different ways, both groups brought a strong sense of patriotism and courage to their decisions.

Stan's brother Walt talked about his brother's decision . . .

> I remember my brother, Stanley, said he was going to meet with our cousin Alice's husband . . . Paul, one of the leaders of the Fair Play Committee. Paul had asked Stan to come over and talk with him, so Stan went. When he came back I asked him what did he say? And he said, Paul explained his position . . . he didn't pressure him at all, in any way. He just told him what they were doing and Stan said . . . 'I kind of agree with them but there are two sides to this . . . there has to be Paul's side . . . and also those that go . . . And I have decided to go.' So, he was supportive of them, but he said he felt he had to go.
>
> *Walter Hayami interview with author, Nov. 4, 2004*

Although he does not write about his decision, we know from his meeting with Paul that Stanley has decided that he would answer his draft call when it came. He had no need to work it out by writing about it. He had made his decision.

At the time of these events, Stan had other, more personal worries as well. His entry on January 24th continues with some serious doubts about his own well-being and his hopes for the future.

Last week I again went to the hospital to try to get an examination but I couldn't get one-too crowded. So today I wrote a letter to them asking if they will not send me a[n] appointment? I have to know what condition my health is in so I can make up my mind about the future. Well it's 11:05 P.M. now so I'd better hit the hay!

According to Walt, Stan had always been very thin and not too strong.

> Stanley in his younger days . . . always seemed like he was undernourished and my mother would keep saying she couldn't feed him enough. We were rather poor, in his early years and she kept saying he didn't get enough milk . . . I can't say he was her favorite, but she worried about him. He worried about him [self] in his diary . . . he was always sure that he had tuberculosis.

January 28, 1944

Well Tomorrow I go to find out about my health. I got a reply to my letter today. I hope nothing is terribly wrong with me. But even if something is wrong with me I feel that I'll be able to take it—no matter how bad.

I've finished reading The Complete Life *by John Erskine and gave a report on it to my teacher today. In his book he says "In order to find happiness, a person should live a complete life." By a complete life he means developing and using all your talents.*

In English class our teacher gave a quotation by Carlyle "Find thy work, there lies your salvation." Miss Sudderth, who is my English teacher, probably was thinking of me when she gave that quotation and when she read off Milton's poem "On his Blindness" in which Milton says approximately this: Every person is put in this world by God to serve a purpose "even those who only stand and wait serve." therefore, even if he is blind, he decides to keep on writing.

Now all this is just adding up to one thing; I too must find my life work soon! My life work should be something that I am not only well equipped for, but one that I like. Now I know what I'd like to be; I'd like to be a combination artist-writer. But I lack confidence in myself. I feel that I wouldn't have enough brains for such a field. I feel that to be a great writer or painter which I would have to be to earn a subsistence in such a field, I would have to be a genius, which means to have an IQ of 140 or over. I only have an IQ of 125.

However I also feel that I may be wrong in thinking this way. I'm still a little wary of I.Q. ratings. When I first went to high school, I had a rating of 95! And then I took a test here and they boosted my I.Q. up to 125. Now I don't know which is right! Maybe neither. Maybe I have a higher I.Q. and perhaps one lower. I took another test the day before yesterday, which may change it again. I feel that I did awful in that test. This last test, though, doesn't seem to me to be a very fair means of determining one's I.Q. It seems to be, more or less, based on accumulative knowledge and not natural intelligence.

And perhaps an I.Q. of 125 isn't bad for a writer or an artist. How would I know—I don't know any artists or writers in person.

Perhaps I am comparing myself with people who are too high an ideal. I read about the old timers such as Leonardo de Vinci, Michelangelo, Plato Plutarch—they are admirable and their I.Q.s are about 170-190-200. But they discourage me. I also hear of these Quiz Kids, and read poems written by high school kids younger than I—and I can't even understand them!

In school work I do O.K. I'm getting all A's in hard subjects such as Solid Geometry and Physics. I've also taken, or I should say, that after I graduate in May I'll have taken 4 and a half years of math, 4 years of science, 4 years of English, 3 and a half years of art, 2 years of Spanish, 1 year of history, 1 year of public speaking, 2 years of gym for a total of 20 and a half credits. I only needed 16 to graduate—I had that amount last June.

Because of all the math & science & art I've taken and because of practicability and respectfulness of it— Frank wants me to be an architect. Well, I've liked and was interested in all the sciences and math I've taken, but I don't like it as much as I do my art and literature. Sure, architecture does have art but I'm afraid its' not the kind that I enjoy—you can't exactly express yourself and create thought stimulating things with architecture. Maybe architecture is something I'd like, however, how should I know?

Now suppose I did become a writer—painter—How high up can I possibly hope to climb? This I wouldn't know, but I do know that whatever field I go into, I'll never be contented with just merely mediocre work—I'd want to the best or nothing! Another thing—I don't really care about how much money I make just so I make enough to be reasonably comfortable and be able to do the things I want to do most.

Some people would say that the math and the science I've taken would be a waste if I went into the art-writing field, but I feel that it would be an asset. Even if I do not use them at all I still feel that my life has been made <u>much</u> richer because I have taken them.

So the question is this: Shall I become a competent and secure architect, which I believe I have enough brains to become, but which I don't believe will satisfy my creative urge very well—Or shall I become a artist -writer, which I very much would like to be, and take a chance on how good I will be. I think that in this field I will also be able to do a little service to mankind. Or will I be just cluttering up the world with more junk. This field would at any rate be more interesting.

I wish I could take an aptitude test. This test will not only determine your interest in a certain field, but also your fitness for such a field.

At one time, not long ago, I wished that I could find my life work in some field which would utilize all my science, math, art, & writing interests. Well I couldn't find such a field, unless it be, writing. But now I feel that it wouldn't be too wise to try to be in too many fields at one time, because:

I   I don't have high enough of an I.Q.

II   Leonardo DaVinci did it, but even he spread himself out too thin.

My heart tells me to be a Artist-writer. My mind tells me to be practical and be someone like an architect.

I'm inclined to follow my heart—not without due reasoning though.

John Erskine says—"Sound reasoning begins in the heart."

My teacher, Miss Sudderth says, and many before her have said so too, that if a person wants to do or be something bad enough—If that person tries hard enough, he will achieve his goal, nothing will then be impossible.

My heart says that if I believe this I will go far.

My mind reminds me that I can indeed go far, but only so far as my I.Q. and race handicap will allow me to go.

Thus you have me—a person who at this moment is quite undecided and uncertain, but who thinks he sees the light and decision springing up ahead.

January 30, 1944—Saturday morning

Today I went to see the doctor. He asked me if I was the one who wrote the letter—and kinda laughed. He asked me why I thought something was wrong with me. I told Dr. Robbins who was the doctor, that I was underweight and felt tired at times. He scoffed and said that most boys around my age are underweight 'cuz they and I've been growing too much. He examined my heart and said "Hell, but you're nervous!" then examined my chest. Before he examined my chest. Before he examined me he sent me to get an x-ray.

Asked me why I wrote the letter. I told him, it was because I wanted to go to college and thought I'd better know if my body will go with me. He said I was perfectly right. Anyway he said I was perfectly all right. Anyway he said for me to come back on Monday to find out my x-ray reading.

I also mentioned my allergic nose to him—he said he'll look after that later.

Jan 31, 1944 NEW LEASE ON LIFE!

Man, do I feel swell! 'member I thought I had T.B. or something, well I don't! Dr. Robbins looked my X-ray over and told me that there's nothing wrong with my lungs—so I guess I'll go on to college! or the army.

And I made up my mind on something else to—I'm going into the artist-writer field. And I'm going to be the best artist in this world (Even if my I.Q. is low.) And another thing, after I graduate from college I'm going to bum my way around the world———So the world better watch out— Hayami is going to the top!

I'd better start building up my body though. I want it to come with me.

Just a little while ago I walked up to the hospital—I was jittery and nervous as hell. By the time I got to the hospital, though, I didn't feel so bad—I tried not to think about it —I felt that this might be the most unhappiest day or the happiest of my life—it turned out to be the most happiest! Dr. Robbins, smoking a long black cigar told me "Nothing there my boy," as he read the x-ray. "You can jump for joy" He extended his hand, but I was so stupefied and so sure that I had T.B. that I forgot to shake it. In fact I walked about a block on the way home before it sank in. Then I looked around—Beautiful day isn't it!—sun shining down on the bright white snow, children yelling and playing—all happiness—no worries!—a future ahead of me!

God has smiled down upon me . . . maybe I'm not worth it. I'm <u>determined</u> to make myself worth it.

ART

Hideo Magara, George Takanashi, Tadao Takano, Sho Kaihatsu,
Miss Joy Krueger, Stanley Hayami

Feb. 2, 1944

Well, yesterday I was elected art editor of the school annual. So I guess I have my work cut out for myself.

Feb 9, 1944

Boy was today cold. Blizzard—windows rattling, wind howling, telephone wires screaming, barrack shaking—snow blowing—bitter cold. When snow is blowing across the ground it looks like carbon dioxide subliming and being blown with a fan . . . not a good illustration, but that's the way it looks . . . drew picture to illustrate.

Feb. 18, 1944

Boy do I have work to do next week is 6 week exams. By next Fri. my staff has to have designs for annual cover ready. Also sketches, all over design for *flyleaf, color scheme, and etc. Guess I'll go sketching tomorrow afternoon.*

I've taken up weight lifting—started last Thursday. Am I weak.

Had to give speech last Tuesday. Didn't have anything ready, but then some queer circumstances things went queer but O.K. Kids say I was hit of show.

Stan's best friend, Tadao Takano, remembers that he had never done pen and ink drawing, but Stan got him started. Several of Tad's large drawings were chosen for the endpapers of the yearbook. According to Tad it was Stan who really introduced him to the world of art and the California artists. Stan also introduced him to the magazine, Art Digest, in the library. He told Tad about the school that his sister Sach was hoping to go to in Chicago, the Institute of Design. He and Stan often discussed going to college one day. Years later, when Tad got out of the service, he managed to attend the Institute of Design. Tad recalls that many of the famous artists who had fled from Europe and the Nazis taught in that school.

Now that Stan has a new lease on life, knows he is not suffering from some terrible disease, he becomes determined to build his strength and stamina. It's at this point that Stanley takes up weightlifting and rigorous body training.

	FEB. 19, 1944	MAY 18, 1944
HT.	5'8"	5'8"
WT.	118 1/8 LBS.	123 LBS.
CHEST (N)	33"	34 1/2"
" (E)	34"	38"
RT. BICEP	9 1/2"	10 1/2"
" " (F)	10 1/2"	11 1/2"
LFT. BICEP	9"	10 1/4"
" " (F)	10"	11 1/8"
NECK	13"	13 1/2"
" (F)	14"	14 1/2"
CALF		13 1/2" 13 3/4"
UPPER LEG		20 1/2" 20 1/8"
PRESS	65 LBS	95 LBS
REP. PRESS	50 X 10	75 X 10
SQUATS	2(60 X 15)	140 LBS X 15 / 150 LBS X 10 / 180 LBS X 5
PULLOVER	15 X 20	25 X 20
LAT. RAISE	5 LBS X 20	12 1/2 LBS X 20
CURLS	2(35 LBS X 10)	3(60 LBS X 10)
ROWING MOTIONS	2(45 LBS X 10)	3(85 LBS X 10)
PRONE PRESS	50 X 10	2(85 LBS. X 14)
BENT ARM PULLOVER	25 X 20	3(40 X 10) AT ONE TIME
TRICEP CURL		50 X 10
DEAD LIFTS		120 X 10
1 ARM ROWING MOTIONS		50 LBS X 10
FOREARM DEVELOPER	1/2 X 5 LBS	2 X 5 LBS.
SPRINGS		10 X 4 STRANDS
ABDOMINAL	10 TIMES 0	15 X 0

Weight lifting classes were one of the most popular pastimes. Stan became serious about working out, building his strength, and keeping detailed records.

Feb. 29, 1944

Got on Heart Mountain Honor roll. Today I received returns on the Ohio Psychological Test. I got a rating of 107 which means that I am in the same group as Phi Beta Kappa students. I should be happy with this result, but I happened to go in there with Tsuneo and Tadao, who happened to place in the top three bracket. Tsuneo got a rating of 129, while Tadao got 128. The highest in the school, got 130, but I don't know who that is. Maybe it's Paul Mayekawa. The test wasn't to determine one's I.Q. however.

Now what I'd like to know is, How much should I depend upon that test? How do I know if it is my true ~~I.Q.~~ intelligence. If I belittle myself and my rating of 107 I will lack confidence in myself. I will say to myself "Oh what's the use." But if I say "To hell with that test, it's not accurate" and go ahead and try my hardest—I'm bound to go far—maybe not as far as I'd like but nevertheless, far.

Now once upon graduating from grammar school, I took such a test. At the time I was given an I.Q. rating of 95. I didn't know this, however, so I studied as hard as I could. Thus I got good grades. At first, they told me I was too dumb to take Algebra, and so I took practical math for a semester. I got five A's and one B the first semester, so I went to see the counselor. He told me they must've made a mistake and let me take algebra, which I found quite easy and fun. Now there's a chance that they've made a mistake on me again—so should I give up, lose fight, lose my ambitions, my confidence, or should I stand up study hard and try to attain my goals nevertheless?

I think I will follow the latter!

Sunday March 25, 1944

Stanley's Homage to Science

Friday night I finished reading about a great negro, George Washington Carver. The story of his life is bound to influence greatly my own.

For one thing I no longer felt satisfied with my former choice of becoming a book illustrator and taking art and literature in college. No, after I read that book I regained my former great love for nature and science and felt that my life would be wasted, so far as being in the service to mankind.

My own feelings and interests and loves fall

remarkably close to Carver's. For one thing, he and I both love nature; secondly, he and I both love and could and can do creative art work; third, we both like science; fourth, he too was handicapped by racial prejudice, only more so than I; fifth, neither of us wanted to or want to make a fortune (I don't base success upon how much money a person has. I want to use money as a means but not as an end in itself.) Sixth, he and I for the most part, have no desire for fame. I believe fame comes to those worthy of it. Not to those who go in search of it. The only diff. between Carver and me was that Carver had brains. Carver was also excellent in music, and that Carver believed firmly in God with heart, soul and mind. (I want to believe in God, I hold him dear in my heart, but doggone it, my mind won't. I pray to God that he will make my mind believe in God also.)

Finally Carver had to make a decision between his love for art and his love for nature and science. He chose nature and science, because he said, "I can help my race best in agriculture."

I too have felt, that I should serve God and Mankind (had something of that sort of in mind on Jan. 31, 1944—last sentence & page Dec 5, 1943.) I too feel that life should have a lofty purposes and reading that book convinced me of this. Wasn't it Edward Bok's mother who said "Edward leave this earth a little more pleasant, a little more beautiful, because you have been in it." And that's just what I'm thinking when I say "I want to leave earth a little more richer than the fertilizer my body is returning to it." Come to think of it, my body is returning what it took out. In other words I should leave some pay for the interest too. I want my life to be constructive not destructive.

So now I wish to heck I can find the hole on earth that I fit in. I wish to find a living where my craving for creative chemurgy (Botanical chemistry or something) and creative art and my longing to serve God and mankind can be satisfied. Carver felt that he couldn't do much unless he concentrated his efforts in one field. Thus he turned to chemurgy and had to stifle his art. I guess it's like a corn stalk; you've got to take the nice suckers off the side so it'll concentrate its growth upward. I also know that DaVinci went into dozens of fields and became great in all—but I know that even he spread himself out too thin. I think that I can let go of my love for literature, but not of either nature or art. So now, before I decide which field to definitely enter I'm going to see which one I'm best, which one I can best serve God. Maybe there isn't yet a definite calling for a man who

Stan is the first one on the list!

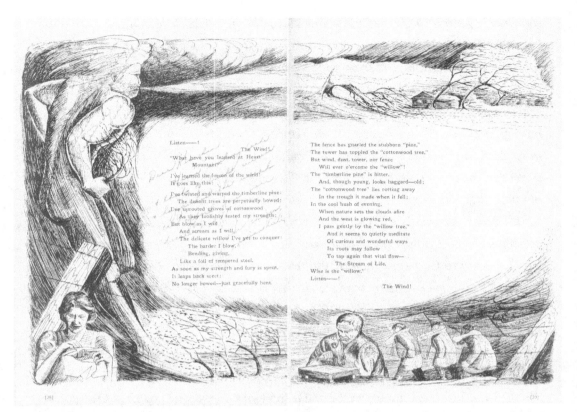

uses creative art and science and yet be of service—but maybe I can create such a position for myself. If I can do that my soul, heart, and mind will be satisfied.

Soul = longing to serve God and mankind to leave something behind for the Progress of Humanity.

Heart = my love of art which I know I will never be able to suffocate.

Mind = my love of science and nature. I call this my equivalent of mind because this is the practical side of me.

Maybe this is too much to ask, maybe I'll be spreading myself out too thin, but I definitely want to live harmoniously with these three. Carver satisfied the 1st and the 3rd but had to stifle his 2nd. I don't think I can do this to any. If I do what he did, I ask "Then why did God give me art as a tool, if he didn't intend for me to use it?" No, I must try to find a hole where my peg of all three will fit in—and if I can't I must choose one way.

Well anyway, I'm ready to go into any field I choose now, except music. The only thing I lack is sufficient brain power.

110

March 24, 1944 10:5 P.M.

Hawaiian guitars playing—
Ukeleles humming—
Warm summer nights,
Crickets creak at the screen door,
Cars in the street not far
Green plants and shrubbery
Eucalyptus trees sighing and

Rustling in a cooling breeze.
Brothers
Sisters and ma and Pa,
Laughter, scoldings and just
*   plain nothing*
These are the thoughts I
*   have tonight.*

While the excitement in camp over the resisters was still bubbling, Frank Hayami has another kind of news for his family . . .

By April of 1944, my friends and neighbors on the local draft board decided that I shouldn't have been classified 4C—why, that man is a native born American, he's not a foreigner—and reclassified me 1A and promptly threw me into a segregated Army unit, training to be a replacement for the 442nd Combat Team which was already in action in the European theatre.

Frank was eventually assigned to Headquarters of the 442nd. Although most of his letters did not survive, some of his army stories are now family legend. It seems that Frank was in training with a good many of the Hawaiian boys who did not like the mainland Nisei. The two groups clashed from the start and frequently settled their disagreements with fists. In fact, the Hawaiian soldiers called the mainland boys "Kotunks"–a word that described the sound that coconuts (and their "empty" heads supposedly) made when they hit the ground. But apparently Frank's head did not hit the ground. When he got into a fist-fight the Hawaiian soldier broke his hand! Frank proudly reported his head was that hard!

All through that spring young men in uniform came home on leave after finishing basic training. Although it is not mentioned in Frank's letter or Stan's diary, there was something so hypocritical about holding visiting soldiers inside of barbed wire fences in order to visit their families before they went off to defend their native land and the flag that flew outside the administration office. They were members of the same US Army as the guards who stood at the gates of the camps that held their families as enemy aliens.

Stan graduated that spring and his buddy, Paul Mayekawa, was the Valedictorian of the class . . .

Valedictory Address: Graduation, May 11, 1944
Citizenship Carries Responsibility by Paul Mayekawa

In the greatest book in the world there is a statement that there is a proper time for everything . . . We are now face to face with a time of graduation from Heart Mountain high school . . . a most opportune time for us to think deeply . . . What are we, you and I?

Are we Japs, simply in a sense as General DeWitt declared, "A Jap is a Jap?" Certainly I admire him for his courage in declaring so plainly an apparently undeniable fact regarding us, but I deplore him for his lack of wisdom and his complete disregard foe Abraham Lincoln's anthem of "goodwill towards all and malice towards none," which even grade school children know by heart and cherish as an ideal for all human beings everywhere in the world.

As evidenced by General DeWitt's remark, there are some Americans who judge us only by our appearances. True, we look no different from regular Japanese because of our blood relations. We have the same pigmentation of the skin and the same physical characteristics, but by right of birth in the United States, we are Americans.

Evacuation has proved, however, that we cannot take citizenship for granted. We, the Japanese-Americans, in not establishing ourselves as firmly in the American way of life as we had thought, must now reaffirm our loyalty to our country and prove ourselves worthy of our citizenship, not by mere words but by our very modes and codes of living.

However, in our eagerness to be true Americans, we should not forsake our Japanese heritage—indeed, this very heritage may be the means by which we . . . further develop and enrich the American culture, for is not America made up of the various cultures of many nations?

Upon graduation, members of this class will disperse and go their separate ways. Some will go to college. Others will relocate and enter again the stream of American life. Wherever they go, each . . . will have a responsibility of representing the Japanese Americans as a whole to the American public, and people will judge us all but the acts of these few.

There are also those among us who will go in to the armed forces. These persons, besides hastening the day of final victory, will constitute what I believe will be the greatest single factor in the re-establishment of the Japanese. Americans in such a definite and permanent place in the American life that issues, such as the evacuation, shall never again be necessary.

Tonight, the night of our graduation from high school, each of us has his own aspirations and hopes for the future, but there is one ideal which I am sure we all have in common—that out of the chaos and disillusion of this war will come a new way of life, such as was described by President Roosevelt in his annual message to Congress on January 6,1941, when he said:

"In future days, which we seek to make secure, we look forward to a world founded upon four essential human freedoms.

"The first is freedom of speech and expression—everywhere in the world.

"The second is freedom of every person to worship God in his own way—everywhere in the world.

"The third is freedom from want–which translated into world terms means economic understandings which will secure every nation a healthy peacetime life for its inhabitants—

Tadao Takano

everywhere in the world.

"The fourth is freedom from fear—which, translated into world terms, means a world-wide reduction of armaments to such a point and in such a thorough fashion that no nation will be in a position to commit an act of physical aggression against any neighbor—anywhere in the world."

But let us remember that the President puts the emphasis upon "eventually" showing that true Democracy is not only a way of life, but also a high ideal yet to be realized. The realization of this ideal can be achieved only by young men and women, who realize the sacredness, the gravity, and the immediacy of the responsibility which goes with living in the most privileged country in the world. With these privileges we acquire the responsibility of caring for less privileged nations of the world.

Remembering that the destiny of the entire human race depends largely upon our attitude toward this sense of responsibility, let this be the dedication of the class of 1944—that we shall, each of us, strive diligently to obtain those true and noble principles of world-wide democracy as stated by our Chief Executive.

Stanley's friend Tad did a glorious drawing (*previous page*) of the birds flying away over the McCullough Mountains that surround the camp, just as so many of the graduates would soon be taking their leave of Heart Mountain.

After graduation Stan continued to keep short and long entries in his diary. There is no date on Stan's booklist, but it is likely he wrote this after he graduated.

BOOKS I HAVE READ IN HIGH SCHOOL

NINTH GRADE
1. STICKEEN — MUIR
2. THOUSAND YEAR PINE — MILLS
3. ADRIFT ON A ICEPAN — GRENFELL
4. BOY'S LIFE ON PRAIRIE — GARLAND
5. BEST SHORT STORIES
6. BOOKER T. WASHINGTON → UP FROM SLAVERY
7. BOYS LIFE OF EDISON
8. LIFE OF HELEN KELLER — HELEN KELLER
9.

1. JAVA HO!
2. CAPE HORN SNORTER
3. KNUTE ROCKNE - MAN BUILDER — STUHLDREYER
4. LAWRENCE OF ARABIA — LOWELL THOMAS
5. AMERICANIZATION OF ED BOK — BY SAME
6. FAR AWAY + LONG AGO — HUDSON
7. FALCONS OF FRANCE — CHARLES NORDOFF
8. LITTLE SHEPHERD OF KINGDOM COME — WILCOX
9. THAR SHE BLOWS!

TENTH GRADE
1. JEKYLL AND HYDE — STEVENSON
2. TALE OF TWO CITIES — DICKENS
3. IVANHOE — SCOTT
4. AS YOU LIKE IT — SHAKESPEARE
5. MERCHANT OF VENICE — SHAKESPEARE
6. ODYSSEY — HOMER
7. THREE MUSKETEERS — DUMAS
8. THE YEARLING — RAWLINGS
9. PEARL LAGOON — CHARLES NORDOFF
10. MEN AGAINST THE SEA — NORDOFF + HALL
11. DARK RIVER — NORDOFF + HALL
12. THE DERILECT — NORDOFF
13. DARK FRIGATE — HAUSE
14. BOY'S INSECT BOOK
15. CARRIBBEAN TREASURE
16. 10,000 LEAGUES OVER THE SEA — ROBINSON
17. MYSTERIOUS ISLAND — VERNE
18. LIFE IN THE ROCKIES — MILLS
19. AUTO. OF MUIR — MUIR
20.

ELEVENTH GRADE

1. ADVENTURES IN
   AMERICAN LITERATURE
2. CROSS CREEK   RAWLINGS
3. BOUNTY TRIOLOGY   NORDOFF & HALL
4. HOW TO WIN FRIENDS
   AND INFLUENCE
   PEOPLE   CARNEGIE
5. GOOD EARTH   PEARL BUCK
6. COUNT VON LUCKNER -
   SEA DEVIL   THOMAS
7. BROTHERS UNDER
   THE SKIN   McWILLIAMS
8. WE TOOK TO THE
   WOODS   D   RICH
9. ONE WORLD   WILLKIE
10. SO YOU WANT to
    BE AN ARTIST
11. VICTORY THRU AIR POWER   SEVERSKY
12. ANIMAL WORLD   DITMARS
13.

12TH GRADE   1943 — 1944

1. GREEN MANSIONS   HUDSON
2. CHADEL   A.J. CRONIN.
3. ANTHONY ADVERSE   HERVEY FILLON
4. The COMPLETE LIFE   JOHN ERSKINE
5. The Stars Look Down   A.J. CRONIN
6. MILL ON THE FLOSS   GEORGE ELIOT
   MARCH 24, 1944
7. GEORGE WASHINGTON CARVER   RAKKHOLM HOLT
8. Random Harvest   JAMES HILTON
9. MEN WHO MAKE THE FUTURE   BRUCE BLIVEN
10. JULY 5, 1944 TREASURY OF SCIENCE   HARLOW SHAPLEY
                                        SAMUEL RAPPORT
                                        HELEN WRIGHT

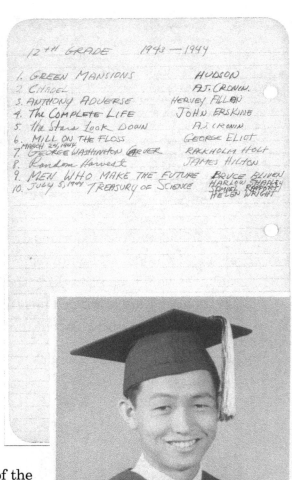

On another page, Stan wrote one of the most curious entries . . .

June 3, 1944

Study further relationship between crystals and Virus's & genes. Perhaps this holds key to secret of life.

From June 3rd to July 20th there are no entries in Stan's Diary. Later he tries to backtrack and record all the events of the weeks that have passed . . .

July 20

Well a lot of things have happened since I last wrote . . .
For one thing I graduated after a fairly tough year. I finished work on the Ht. Mt Annual. [Yearbook]

114

On May 30 I left for Denver and took my army induction physical exam on June 1. The amazing thing is I actually passed! After taking the exam Mits Kawashima, Calvin Kawanami, Lloyd Kitozono and Mas—& I roamed around town, ate a big T. bone steak, saw Guadacanal Diary then we went to a hotel to sleep. The next day (June 2) I woke up shivering, as I went to bed in my shorts only as I didn't bring my pajamas, and it was snowing outside to my amazement. After eating another steak with Mits and the other guys I went tramping thru the slush down Larimer street and then over a long bridge and finally to Obasan & Ojisan's house.

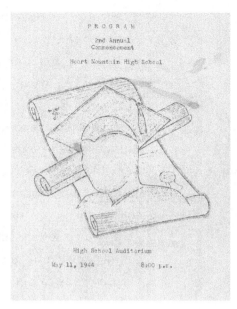

Heart Mt. Wyo   *August 20, 1944*

Well its been a very long time since I last wrote. Things have happened too. First of all Frank went into the army (he's been in for about 3 months now.) Then around May I went to Denver and took my army physical which I passed! (Surprised me.) While I was in Denver I stayed with Obasan and Ojisan for a day. I played with Polito and met Catheryn and Alice and Amson.

About 2 weeks after taking my physical, I graduated high school. We had caps and gowns and all—ceremony took place in the gym-aud.

After graduation I loafed around awhile and then around May 26 Tsuneo

Printed on a mimeograph machine, this is the program for Stan's graduation.

Hiyake, Tadao Takano, Walter and I went out to Hardin Mont. to work. Thinning beets was our job and it proved quite tough, but soon I got used to it. After about a week Tad and Tsuneo wanted to go home, I wanted to stick it out until I was inducted. The relocation officer told them they couldn't leave. I got quite disgusted with them at times because of their laziness.

Stan's Work Permit Card, his official ID, when he left for Montana.

Stan must have left his diary at home, but he wrote a few letters from Montana that included some line drawings of their housing. Since Stan uses no Japanese in his diary, his first letter home comes as a surprise, because it is written in large part in Japanese. We know him only from his diary, which is written entirely in English. His letters reveal that Stan was bilingual, at least somewhat.

In his letters to his parents, Stanley writes in a mix of English and Japanese. Like most Nisei, he was most accustomed to writing in English, but he was able to speak and write to his parents in Romaji a form of Japanese written with Roman letters. Stan was not a student of this language and his usage was not scholarly or intended for publication.

It was a loving son's way of communicating directly to his parents in the language they could read. His use of *Romaji* gives us a glimpse into the messages Stanley sent to his family.

Sat. June 3, 1944
Hardin, Mont.

Dear Pa & Ma:
Thank you very much for your tegami [letter]. Boku nankashi kyo *rest* shimashiteru no *[I am resting today]*. Ame ga hidoku fu[t]teru no *[It is raining very hard]*. *Most day[s] very hot.*

All this week we worked very hard. We worked from 5 to 11:30 and from 2 to 7:30. About 11 hours a day or more. Every morning 5 oclock ni okiru no *[get up at] 2 hour* gur[a]i tabete [so]no ato *rest* shimasu no *[eat and then rest for about 2 hrs]*. 8 ka 9 gur[a]i ni neru no *[I go to bed around 8 or 9]*. Asobu toki shitotsu mo n[a]i *[No time to play at all]*.

5 o'clock	okiru no *[get up]*
6 o'clock	hatarakimasu no *[work]*
11:30	*stop work*
12	*eat*
12:30	*rest*
2	*start work again*
7:30	*stop working*
8	*eat*
8:30 or 9	*sleep*

Kono shigoto wa senaka ni totemo er[a]i *[This work is very hard on my back].* Boku nankashi wa totemo slow *[na]*no desu *[I am very slow]*—soshite-mo *"each"* s[hi]to wa *$6.50 a day* tsukuru no *[But each of us earns about $6.50 a day].*

Tadao to Tsuneo mo shigoto [ni] [a]ide k[a]iri t[a]i no desu *[Tadao and Tsuneo have already lost interest in the work and want to go home].* Boku to Mitsuru demo *"work"* sukiden[a]i demo mada *3 week* gur[a]i *stay* shit[a]i no *(Me and Mitsuo [Walt] do not like this work either, but [we] still want to stay about 3 more weeks).* So demo are nankashi k[a]iru no dat[t]araba Walter to boku demo k[a]iran to dame *[So, but if they go home, either Walter and me or [somebody else] must go home].* Are nankashi k[a]irit[a]i no desu wa *[They want to go home].*

1. fresh vegetables n[a]i *[There are no fresh vegetables].* Taberu mono amashi e de n[a]i *[Food is not very good].*

2. Homesick

3. hard work

4. enough sleep n[a]i *[No enough sleep]*

Maybe are nanka k[a]it[t]e mo Mitsuru to boku wa *3 weeks* gur[a]i *"more" stay* suru *[Even if they go home, Walter and I will stay three more weeks].*

Boku nanka re(?) de boku ga ichiban hayai no desu *[[In our group] I am the fastest].* Mitsuru ga ichiban slow *[na]* no *[Walter is the slowest].*

Every day motto hayaku narioru node motto hayaku *"go home"* dekeru *[Since every day [we] are getting faster, [we] can go home even faster[.*

Kyo farmer ga *"town"* ni boku nanka tsurete iku no *[Today the farmer is taking us to town].*

Farmer wa tottemo e shito desu, so dakkara *"quit"* shi taku n[a]i *[Farmer is a very good person so I don't want to quit].*

Boku nankashi *nice 3 room house* ni sunderu no *[We live in a nice 3 room house].*

Benjo wa amashi e de n[a]i. *"outside"* ni aru no *[Toilet is not very nice. It is outside].*

Benjo *[Toilet]*

Ko[n]nani hataraku no *[We work like this].*

House
Well next time motto kakimasu *[I will write more].*

Love,
Stanley

Although Stan tells his parents in his June 3rd letter that he expects to stay another three weeks, by June 5th, just two days later, he has had enough of farming. He is ready to return to Heart Mountain, but he must ask permission of O. Leon Anderson, his Relocation Officer. Stan's handwritten letter explains that he expects to be called to active duty any day. Then he made a mistake of writing . . . "I do not feel that thinning beets is exactly the most enjoyable way to spend my last few days before going into the army." He asks for permission for both himself and Walter.

The very next day they had a nasty reply from the United States Department of the Interior in Billings, Montana.

Gentlemen:

This letter is in reply to your letter…you are of course aware of the man power shortage which exists throughout the United States. You are also aware of the fact that agricultural production must be maintained—crops must be cared for whether any has a good time or not.

While I realize that you desire to spend the remaining time before induction with your parents, friends, and relatives, I am reluctant to take action on your case without further investigation.

It has been my observation that considerable time has usually elapsed before draftees who have passed their physical are called. Also, without exception, Japanese Americans are not called as rapidly as are other draftees. Therefore, I am quite sure that it will be sometime before you are called and you are not in any great emergency with regard to your release.

You are under contract to do a job in agriculture. I believe you will have ample time to complete your thinning job at least. Therefore, please stay on the job until I have been able to come and see you. I hope to be able to come the last of this week or the first of next week. Until I see you then, stay in and "pitch" on your present assignment. The boys on the invasion crew are not having too good a time.

Sincerely,
O. Leon Anderson, Relocation Officer

Mr. Anderson's stern letter turned out to be wrong. The army was in need of replacements—the sooner the better. Stan wrote to his parents just days later...

Sat June 10, 1944

Dear Pa & Ma

Got notice from draft boards to go to army induction June 19. So boku wa next Saturday, June 17, ni k[a]i ru [So, I will go home next Saturday, June 17]. I think Walter is going to come home the same time. We were going to try to come home last week, but the relocation officer in Billings said no.

Work isn't too hard for us now that we are used to it. My hands are very tough now. Gasa gasa desu [[They] are rough].

Kyo no afternoon boku nankashi Hardin ni iku no—aso bi ni (I will go to Hardin this afternoon to have fun.

Love, Stanley

Stan later writes more stories about farming as he continues to catch up in his diary . . .

Aug. 20, 1944

On the thinning of sugar beets I usually did a bit more than they, and then of the chores there were to do I had to do most of them. In the morning I usually had to wake them up and then run to the farmhouse to get the milk. Many times I returned to find them still sleeping so I had to start the fire going too. After all meals I had I always washed the dishes, no [one] ever helped me. Then at noon Walt went home early to cook then about an hour later we went home. As soon as we got home Tsuneo and Tadao usually went right to bed and rest. So I had to go get bucket full of water. I usually helped Walt with the cooking. After eating they went right back to bed again while I washed dishes and pans for at least another half hour. After resting for about an hour I woke them up and went to work. We worked until about 7 o'clock, and, boy, it was really hot in the afternoon! At night I usually chopped some wood as Tad & Tsuneo were back in bed after meals I had to wash dishes and pots and pans for another half hour while the rest were already asleep or resting in bed. So while I didn't care too much about the thinning of beets I sure didn't think much about the unfair division of chores. All Tsuneo and Tad did were to bring in drinking water about once a week, occasionally to get buckets of dish washing water (This when they did do it, they considered a favor to me) and a little more often but not more than I, they shared in the wood chopping. Tsuneo's job was to lay in bed and the book keeping.

Therefore I was a little happy when my induction notice came and after getting our $75 apiece from our genial boss, Mr. Groskoff, Walt & I left Hardin on the 17th of June. Walter, who I thought would be the laziest did a good job which I was proud of. He was much slower than the rest of us on thinning, but he was also much more thorough. Walter also did the hard job of cooking, which the others felt was quite easy. He also was very cheerful at all times which helped quite a bit. I never asked Tsuneo and Tadao how they liked the chores after we left, but they told us that hoeing which is supposed to be much easier than thinning proved to be much harder for them. I think that doing chores for a change had something to do with its being harder.

At any rate I returned home & gave Pa & Ma each $15 which made them very happy & me doubly so. I went to Fort Logan for induction and returned all the next week.

All this whole time, except for the time I was at Hardin, I have been going steadily to weightlifting, even to this day. I have gradually improved in strength, health and appearance. I'm positive that if I keep at it I will soon have a superior body and likewise in strength.

Tsuneo and Tadao reached home about last month and I have forgiven them in my mind for their laziness. We have been good friends throughout and have gone weightlifting together.

I have also gone swimming about every single afternoon since returning from my induction some 8 weeks ago. After much practice I learned how to swim.

So that brings me up to the present day Sunday, Aug. 20, 1944.

[More]Aug. 20, 1944

Today is a beautiful morning. Up and down our barrack I can hear kids *playing, doors opening and closing. Radio speaking in the barrack across from me. Pop's over at the* sho gi *room [A game like chess.] I guess—he's supposed to work out this morning with the dumbbells he received two weeks ago from York. Walt's still in bed sleeping, he went to our block social last night. Gee I sure wish I could dance—I guess it's like anything else—you got to drive yourself and learn—no use sitting and wishing. Momo [mother] is probably washing clothes. I wonder how Grace [Sach] is over in New York—*

Many older men played ancient games such as ShoGi and Goh.

haven't seen her now for a year, she's taking psychology & math at Hunter College. Her birthday is next week—good thing I sent her a present already. I guess Frank's at that picnic over at Shelby today.

Well the reason I'm writing again after such a long lapse is because around next Tuesday I'm going to go to active duty. Probably this shall be the last time I will write in this book in a long time.

Perhaps I should also go over some of the news that has happened in the last 3 months. Well France has been invaded and the allies are now close to Paris. Saipan Island in the South Pacific has been taken with the result that Premier Tojo and his entire staff was forced to quit.

Hitler has been almost killed. In Italy the Japanese-American are doing a wonderful job. The 100th is the most decorated outfit in the army. Willie wrote from someplace in Italy. Hasn't seen action yet, Two of last year's volunteers from our camp have already met their death.

Heart Mt. has been a dead place, a wonderfully live place too. Dust has blown through it and snow storms too. Someday, from a foreign battlefield I shall remember it with homesickness. Mother, Father, brothers, sister, friends, mess hall, movie theatres, ice skating, swimming, school, weightlifting—all shall try to well up in my throat at once.

<u>*Aloha*</u>

Stanley Hayami

Aug. 21, 1944

Tonight is my last night here in camp. I'm leaving for the Army tomorrow morning. I'm leaving on approximately the same day that I got here some two years ago, Aug. 2, 194[2]

I remember that day very well—it was hot and dusty when the train pulled in next to the warehouses (we thought they were to be our barracks. We looked outside and there were a stack of Pomona kids I knew, helping to take care of our baggage! It sure felt funny seeing people you knew after traveling some thousand miles.

The docs looked us over and then we were loaded on trucks and driven to our assigned barracks. On the way, people lining the street yelled at us to greet us. I remember seeing George Azuma sitting under a telephone pole.

Well all this is past and memories now—I met a lot of good friends here in camp—There's Tsuneo, Tadao, George, Tomo, Paul Mayekawa, Hiroshi K., Kunio Y., Sab Naguno, Jim Yada & Nakada.

It'll be fun to see all these people again after years have gone by. I wonder how much Tsuneo, Tadao and George will have improved in their physics [physiques] and their strength. George already presses 125 and only weighs 120. I wonder what sort of future scientists and artists they'll make.

Well only time will tell right now I've gotta get some shut eye—gotta get up early tomorrow.

Hope Ma & Pa & Walt & Sach & Frank all stay in sound health and are happy always.

Aloha til I write again—It may be a year it may be sooner- (I hope) or maybe ten years (groan).

****

EIGHT — HEART MOUNTAIN SENTINEL

27 Residents Report for Active Duty

Men Called From Center Total 123

Twenty - seven enlisted reservists, largest contingent ordered to report to date from Heart Mountain, left Tuesday for active duty in the army with Ft. Logan, Colo., as their destination. The group boosts to 123 the number of local youths called for active service since the reinstitution of selective service procedures for nisei.

Those who departed were Pvt. Herbert Endo, 7-14-C; Pvt. Toshihumi Hanada, 24-2-B; Pvt. Stanley K. Hayami, 8-2-B; Pvt. Fumio Higashihara, 6-5-B; Pvt. Karuo Horiuchi, 14-19-C; Pvt. Minoru Horiuchi, 14-19-C; Pvt. Keiji Iko, 21-23-D; Pvt. Kaoru

Successfull Relocation Program Being Carried Out in Dayton

How the resettlement program is being carried out successfully in the city of Dayton, Ohio, with the help of a nisei was told in the monthly report of the Church federation of Dayton and Montgomery county on the resettlement of Japanese Americans.

On an invitation from G. Raymond Booth, relocation officer of the Cincinnati area, Yosh Kodama, former executive secretary of the relocation planning commission at Heart Mountain, was called to explore relocation possibilities in the area and possibly develop a resettlement program in Dayton.

Kodama met with the committee on Japanese American relocation early in May this year and in June he accepted a position with the Church federation

constant average cost of living, and there were 24 industrial concerns with national reputation providing ample employment opportunities.

The resettlement committee made systematic contacts, concentrating on three fields of action: the churches—for reception and acceptable community sentiment particularly in small communities and in good neighborhoods near available war housing; industries—both management and labor leaders, for employment and economic equality; the federal and metropolitan housing agencies—for temporary and permanent housing of evacuees.

As the program progressed, congregations of various churches, women's groups, classes, businessmen and clubs asked for

Elementary Schools to Open Sept. 4

School bells will ring once again for approximately 960 grade school youngsters as the new fall semester opens Sept. 4. Pupils residing in blocks 1 to 15 are to report to Washington school in block 7, while those living in blocks 17 to 30 will attend the Lincoln school in block 25, according to Howard D. Bugbee, principal of the elementary schools.

Students who have not attended school in Heart Mountain previously are to report to the principal's office in 25-7 with report cards from the last school attended.

Stanley reported for duty at Fort Logan, Colorado on August 22, 1944. For the first time in two and a half years he was no longer a prisoner; he was as "free" as any soldier can be.

BEYOND THE DIARY

Camp Blanding, Fla.
Sept. 6, 1944

Dear Pa, Ma, & Walt,

I got here yesterday afternoon and am OK. Camp Blanding, Florida is hot!!! Sweat like heck.

We left Logan on the 1st. Traveled through Omaha, Neb., Iowa, Chicago, Indiana, Ohio, Kentucky, Knoxville, Tenn., Georgia, & Florida.

We stopped in Cincinatti for about 5 hrs. but I wasn't able to call Eddie up, cuz I didn't know his phone number. They didn't tell us where we were going until so I didn't know whether I was going to Shelby or here until we passed Cincinatti.

Took us four days to get here. Today was our first full day and already they had us drill all morning and then th dril they gave us our

We

Note:

Soldiers were not generally allowed to keep diaries in combat zones as they might reveal secrets to the enemy if captured. Stanley left his diary at home. From this point on we depend on Stanley's letters home to hear his voice. Fortunately, he continued to find time to write home and his family kept those letters as treasures they generously share in the pages that follow.

Private Stanley Hayami

Private Stanley Hayami reported for duty at Fort Logan, a reception center about six miles outside of Denver, Colorado. About a week later, on the 28th of August 1944 the Hayami family received an envelope with forms that Stanley had signed, allotting part of his monthly paychecks for life insurance, making his mother the beneficiary, and for Defense Bonds bought in the name of his sister, Grace (Sach), and his brother, Frank.

Several weeks passed before Stan's first letter arrived in Wyoming. He was no longer in Colorado. Nor was he with the majority of Japanese American recruits, who typically did basic training at Camp Shelby in Mississippi. Stanley and his buddies were sent to Camp Blanding in Florida. There was no way Stan could call his family at Heart Mountain. The Nikkei had no phone service inside the camp. Letters and telegrams were the only way to communicate and Stan, being Stan, wrote home pretty frequently.

Camp Blanding, Fla.
Sept. 6, 1944

Dear Pa, Ma, & Walt,

I got here yesterday afternoon and am OK. Camp Blanding, Florida is hot!!! Sweat like heck.

We left Logan on the 1st. Traveled through Omaha, Neb. Iowa, Chicago, Indiana, Ohio, Kentucky, Knoxville, Tenn., Georgia, and Florida.

We stopped in Cincinnati for about 5 hrs, but I wasn't able to call Eddie up 'cuz I didn't know his phone number.

They didn't tell us where we were going so I didn't know whether I was going to Shelby or here until we passed Cincinnati. Took us four days to get here.

Today was only our first full day and already they had us drill all morning and then this afternoon they gave us our rifles. I spent most of the day cleaning it.

We go to sleep here at 9 and wake at 5 & it's so hot that even at nite I sweat and I have to sleep in my shorts without blankets.

I live in a hut with four other kids—five altogether. They're all nice kids.

There's supposed to be quite a few Japanese kids here from Heart Mt., but I haven't seen any yet.

Well I got to go to sleep pretty soon so—until I write again.

Love
Stanley

PS Hope everyone at home is O.K.

UNITED STATES ARMY

Fort Blanding, FLa.
UNDATED

Dear Ma, Pa, & Walt,

Please send me about four clothes hangers.

Did you get the letter I sent yesterday? I still haven't got a pen so I'm borrowing other kid's pens, but I have asked Sach to send me one.

Today was hot again—we drilled all morning and didn't do much this afternoon. It's cool tonite though.

Well, Pa, are you still issho kemme *[very hard] exercising? I've been thinking that since you are old, you had better take it easy, be slow in using heavier weights. Don't increase the weights until you can easily do the exercise the required number of times. When you increase the weight do half or less repetitions as before.*

<u>*Never strain*</u>. Muri shinan na *[Do not overwork yourself] its very bad for the heart.*

<u>*Exercise slowly and easily*</u>. *When I say exercise slowly, I mean for you to bring the weight up slowly and down slowly. In that way your muscles will get the most good. I say easily, because if you do the exercise slowly, you naturally cannot do as many reps and if it isn't easy to bring the weights up, don't. Anyway, all I'm trying to say is don't strain.*

If you get tired after an exercise, rest five minutes or so before doing the next one. Boku wa mada *exercise* shite nai *[I have not done any exercise yet]. I haven't even found the lifting room yet. Anyway Pa, are you feeling more* shik[k]ari *[strong and healthy]? That's the main idea. How's your stomach?*

How about the rest? How's school ma? Has school opened yet? Walt.

I'm feeling O.K. I haven't much more to say so good nite. Boku wa nemu tai *[I am sleepy].*

It may seem surprising that these sections in Japanese were not censored as suspicious. During wartime, letters to and from GIs typically arrived with words, sentences and even paragraphs cut out. Sometimes letters arrived looking like Swiss cheese with words cut out all over the page. However, in the 442nd, the job of censoring mail was assigned to Japanese speaking soldiers who were able to understand both languages.

Stanley comments from time to time about censoring himself, not being able to say where he is or exactly what he is doing. His letters focus on everyday things he needs or hopes to do. While his diary entries were sometimes playful dreams of the future, the letters are down to earth.

If Stanley is worrying, he is not writing home about his concerns.

It is almost as if he is trying to calm his parents as well as himself.

Bodybuilding has become a passion to Stanley. His advice to his father is both wise and endearing. He's very protective of his dad's well being. Stan was ahead of his time with his enthusiasm for exercising. It sounds like he invented the pro-active fitness mindset that is as current as today's health advocates.

Camp Blanding, Fla.
Sept 17, 1944

Dear Folks,

Bokku wa *O.K.* desu *[I am O.K.]. Kyo [today] is Sunday and I get a rest. All week was hard, but others say we haven't done anything yet. Weather is getting cool and so it is easier.*

127

I couldn't get dependency allowance. But I guess Frank can.

I'm going to have $20 of my pay sent home every month which I want you to save for me. I will need lots of money to go home with when I get a furlough because Blanding is so far from home.

My expenses will be for every month:

1 pay to be sent home	*$20.00*
2 War bonds	*$7.50*
3 insurance	*$6.50*
4 laundry	*$1.50*
Total	*$35.50*
left	*$14.50*

That means bokku wa *[I will have] $14.50 every month spend* suru *[to spend].*

So far I've only gotten one letter and that's from Sach.

I guess New York is closer to here than Heart Mt.

I hope you are all O.K. and in good health.

How's school Walt? What are you doing Ma & Pa? Madda shishu *to English class* ikkioru *[Are you still going to embroidery and English class]?* Papa madda sage(?)oru *and* shogi asonderu no *[Papa are you still exercising and playing* shogi*]?*

Well that's all for now

Love

Stanley

PS Hope you can read this letter. I'm writing with air-mail so please tell me how long it takes to get there. Did you send me my hangers yet?

Camp Blanding, Fla.
Sept. 24, 1944

Dear Folks,

I got your letters, thank you so much. Mama your letter was very good.

It's still hot here and army is very tough. I'm getting used to it though, I think.

Walt, How come you don't write me?

I got the coat hangers last week, thanks.

Tonite I've gotta walk guard at one o'clock 'til 3 o'clock so, I gotta get me some sleep. Tomorrow we're going to have a hard day.

Sach sent me this pen last week.

Frank wrote me a letter too. He says he's going to go to Radio School— good, don't you think so?

I hope Heart Mt. isn't too cold. I hope everyone is O.K. at home.

Walt, Max Koga is here. Yone left here about a week before I got here.

I've been going weight lifting regularly for the last two weeks. I go by myself since no one else seems to want to go.

Well I guess I'd better catch some sleep.

トテモ　ネムイ　デス
to te mo　NE MU i　DE su

Totemo nemui desu *[I am very sleepy]*

Love your son & brother

クニオ

PS send me my gym shorts please, also my bathing suit & jock strap.

Most envelopes say to Hayami Family but the next envelope is addressed to Mr & Mrs Hayami & 1 Son . . . a bit of humor. Indeed, Walt is the only son left with his family. Stanley starts his letter by praising his mother's writing skill. Like other Issei, Stanley's mother started attending English classes soon after she arrived at Heart Mountain. Although we do not have her letters, it seems likely that she expressed concern about the way she writes English, because Stanley makes a point of being most supportive, praising her writing. As time passed, more mothers and fathers attended English classes so that they could write to and read letters from their sons and daughters who were "outside," working at jobs, or in the service.

Not surprisingly, most of Stan's letters are dated on a Sunday. That was the only day of the week Stan would have had time to catch up with his writing.

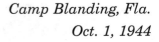

Camp Blanding, Fla.
Oct. 1, 1944

Dear Pa, Ma, & Walt,

I got your letters—thank you. I'm O.K. and in good health. I'm glad to hear you're OK too.

Today is Sunday so I'm taking it easy. All last week was hard and hot, but I guess the hard part is still coming. We learned how to crawl thru sand on our bellies—sure feels bad—hot, sweaty and sand sticking all over you. I'm learning a lot in classes too (that's right, feels like school.) We do a lot of other things, but as I said before, I'm not supposed to write much about my training here.

Yesterday, Sat. (we always have afternoon off on Saturdays) I went swimming from 1 PM until 2:30 and went weight lifting from 3:00 till 4:30 and then I ate dinner and saw a movie at nite. I've been going weight lifting 2 time a week (usually Wednesday and Saturday). I haven't gained any strength or any weights yet—this soldier's life just seems to wear me out—anyway I haven't lost any weight. The food here is pretty good and I usually get an ???? (okawari [second]). It's so hot here and we sweat so much that everyone usually drinks about 3 or 4 glasses of water at each meal.

Right now Sunday afternoon—camp is pretty empty 'cuz everyone went to see a movie or went to towns around here. There's Jacksonville, St. Augustine, and some other town around here. St Augustine is supposed to be the oldest town in America.

This morning I woke up late, 7 o'clock (usually we have to wake up 5 or 6) and ate breakfast and then went back to bed til 9. I did my laundry after that (I send some of my clothes to the laundry (Laundry only costs $1.50 a month for any no. of clothes.) but I have to wash clothes like stockings, shorts, shorts, towels and such, because I don't have enough to change into. (laundry takes a week.)

So if you have a couple of extra plain white towels could you please send them to me? (Don't have to be plain white but it's better if they are.) Also could you send me those steel cables that Frank sent from N.Y. I haven't asked him if I could use them, but I guess he won't mind. If he ever needs them I will send them to him from here. While you are at it, you may as well send me my

*Calculus book and slide rule. I have practically no time to study, but I might
make some time to do it. I hope that's all I'll ever have to ask you to send me-
I know it's a lot of trouble and time to send.*

So here's the list of things I asked for:

> *towels*
>
> *steel cables*
>
> *calculus book*
>
> *slide rule*

*By the way have you sent my other things I asked for . . . bathing suit,
gym shorts, and etc? If you haven't, send them together with this stuff.*

*Well I hope everything is O.K. at home. Did you go to Powell? Walt, your
handwriting is very good now (mine sure ain't). After hearing from Tsuneo
and Tadao about them going to college I sure am J [jealous]. Hope you are
exercising, Pa. Best time to exercise in wintertime.*

Mama, ナニシマテルノ *(what are you doing)? Yo ma re ru (Can you
read this)?*

Sach wrote me a long letter yesterday—she seems to be O.K. too.

Don't worry Papa and Mama I try to treat my friends whenever I can.

*Pa and Ma you both write very good letters for Issei. My friends are sure
surprised.*

Well, take care of yourselves.

マダサムクナタカ *(Has it gotten cold yet)*

マタベルモノドナデス *(How is the food)?*

サヨナラ

Goodby

Aloha

Adios

So Long

> *Your son & brother*
> *Stanley*

P.S. I got the hangers O.K. Thank you very much.

As usual, Stan writes about being careful with his money. His buddies seem
to be going to town on the weekend, but Stan is staying on the base, maybe to

save money. He assures the family that having the laundry done is inexpensive. Yet it seems worth commenting on.

Stan's brother, Walt, recalled that Stan was always skinny and his mother worried about Stanley's health. While he was in Heart Mountain, Stan worried about his health, too. Now as he faces the rigors of basic training and the battlefields to come, getting strong had to become all the more urgent. Eating seconds and lifting weights was one way for Stan bolster his sense of well being and in writing home, he is assuring his mother that he is doing all right.

The Hayamis wasted no time in getting Stan's requests into the mail. In a little more than the two weeks it took for a package to arrive, Stanley writes a letter of thanks . . .

[no location given]
Oct. 18, 1944

Dear Pa, Ma, & Walt,

Thank you very much for my stuff.—it all came in tact.

Last nite and tonite I was on guard duty so I'm pretty sleepy. Last nite I had the 4th shift, 1:00 to 3:00 in the morning. It was quiet and dark and nothing ever happened while I walked my post carrying my rifle on my shoulder. Tottemo t[a]igi dat[t]a [It was very hard]. Tonite I had it easy I watched the P.X. [post exchange- a kind of store] this afternoon 5:00 to 7:00. I won't have to pull guard again for about another two weeks.

I'm going to get a <u>sharpshooters</u> medal for shooting a rifle I think. But that's nothing in my company, we have almost 60 expert shooters, about 80 sharpshooters and the rest were marksmen. I think that maybe our company broke the record or something in this camp. Everyone in our company will get a medal.

We have a very nice Captain here. He hardly ever bawls us out. We also have two good lieutenants. One fought against the Japanese in the Solomon's but he sure is nice to us. The other one taught the 442nd and thinks a hell of a lot of us.

But—we have one lousy lieutenant, he's smart as heck, but boy does he cuss and bawl us out. He makes us feel like we're the worse soldiers in the army. But, I guess he just wants to keep us from getting cocky. He's bawled the heck out of me so many times that I haven't counted. He's going to leave soon and now I'm almost sorry—I was getting used to being bawled out by him.

Well it's lights out soon so thanks for the stuff and for the letters Pa, Ma &

Walt. Mama I can read your letters very good—all of the letters were good in fact. Thanks!

Love,
Stanley

Stanley's letter about his sharpshooter medal is reminiscent of his student days. By nature Stan was very competitive about his grades and although he was a good student, he often compared himself less than favorably to others. Now in the Army, Stan is once again less than thrilled with his performance. On the other hand, he acknowledges that there are poorer shots than he is.

His comments about the officer bawling him out seems like an unusual circumstance for Stan, but quite typical of tough officers and sergeants who had to turn green recruits into soldiers during their rigorous basic training. Young soldiers often felt a mix of respect and resentment toward their demanding leaders who were getting them ready for battle. With a few exceptions, the officers leading the all-Nisei 442nd were Caucasians. The exceptions were a few Nisei officers who'd served in the ROTC or with the Territorial Guard of Hawaii. African American segregated units also had mostly Caucasian officers. Another example of the racist bias minorities faced in the US Army of World War II.

Oct 22, 1944

Dear Walt,

Happy Birthday!

I'm sending you a present—it isn't much, but I couldn't get anything here in camp. A friend of mine went out of camp to get it. I wanted to get you something musical, but he said he couldn't even find one music shop.

I'm O.K.—today's Sunday so I'm loafing around. I've already done my wash and cleaned my shoes. I'll go to the main post office today and send your present.

Well I hope you're all O.K. I gottta go eat now.

Love,
Stan

Dear Folks,

Dona des ka [How are you]?

It's late and I'm tired so I won't write much tonite.

Yesterday I went on nite problems again. Got up at 5 AM and went to bed at 3 AM the next morning. Woke up 8 o'clock this morning—that's why I'm tired.

Wasn't hard as last time though—last time we crawled through streams under barb wire, through swamps, crossed rivers up to our waist, got all wet and cold then walked the 5 mi. back home. This time we didn't get wet at all.

Today I got my sharpshooter's medal, but I don't feel like wearing it. In a regular hakujin [Caucasian] company a sharpshooter is rated very high, but in our company it is doing just average. In fact it is doing below average because almost half of our company got experts medal. Just a very few got marksman medal which is the worst. In fact our company did so damn good that we broke the Camp Blanding record! Our company did the best in Camp Blanding History!

Well I haven't too much to say tonite. I hope you're all alright Pa, Ma, and Walt. Hope it doesn't get too cold.

Has Frank written from wherever he is now? He hasn't written me for a long time.

Sach writes about once a week.

Walt did you get what I sent you?

I'm sending a pamphlet or something which the Army told me to send home. It shows what kind of training I'm getting.

"Army" wa amashi "hard" de nai [Army is not very hard]. Boku wa "used to" nare oru [I am used to it].

I lost 2 ? lbs. so far, but hakujins [Caucasians] say that they started gaining weight after the 7th week. I hope so, because we're starting our 8th week now. I exercise with the springs every other day and go to weight lifting room only once a week now.

Well take care of yourselves.

Stanley

This is the first of several letters in which Stanley begins asking about his brother Frank. He knew Frank had to be almost finished with his basic training.

That meant he would be shipped overseas soon. Before leaving for the battlefields of Europe, Frank would be allowed to go visit the family in Wyoming. But Stan can't seem to get word about Frank's whereabouts. It's in this letter that Stanley writes that he's pretty far along with his own his basic training and expects to see them in late January.

Once again Stanley writes proudly about the superiority of his company. He was not merely boasting. Nisei soldiers were determined to be outstanding. It's often said that they had more to prove than others. They not only had to fight the enemy abroad, they needed to show the nation that they were 100% Americans. This expression, "100%—even 200% American" was widely used—it says they are American, not Japanese. As they left their families, it was not uncommon for parents to send them off with words meant to instill courage and a willingness to face whatever waited on the battlefield. They were told, "Bring no shame to your family."

In time, the young men of the 442nd Regimental Combat Team would make Army history. 13,500 Nisei men from all ten relocation centers served in the U.S. Army. All together more than 33,000 Nisei served in WWII. This includes those in the 100th and 442nd, Military Intelligence Service, the Women's Army Corps (WAC), Nurses Corp, Occupation Forces in Japan and Europe, and others. (Source: National Japanese American Memorial Foundation)

On a day-to-day basis, young men like Stanley faced the realities of military life. Time was measured in the weeks of basic training and harsh conditions that were meant to toughen them up for whatever awaited them across the ocean. Stanley reports about the cold, but he knows from experience that Heart Mountain is colder! In this and other letters he reassures his parents that he is getting along. Complaining about his circumstances is not Stan's style.

Nov. 5, 1944

Dear Folks,

 Thanks for the letter, Walt.

 I'm O.K. and Camp Blanding is pretty cool now so I feel good, too. By the way I'm half finished with my basic training now.

 Friday nite we slept outside—was a little chilly, but otherwise it was alright.

 Well I hope everyone is alright. Is Heart Mt. getting cold? What are you doing Pa & Ma? Are you all exercising yet?

How is Frank and where is he right now He told me he was going to go to radio school and then he stopped writing. Guess he ought to be home on furlough pretty soon.

Well today is Sunday and I'm going to try to take it easy.

Love
Stanley

St Augustine, Fla.
Nov. 19, 1944

Dear Pa, Ma, & Walt,

Well I'm O.K. and feeling fine.

Today for the first time I left camp. (Everyone else has left camp at least 5 times, but I never felt like it.) I'm here in St. Augustine, which is the oldest town in the United States.

It has an old fort here, which was built back in 1590 or so. I visited that place in the morning.

I went to the beach in the afternoon (by the way I came with another fellow named Henry Ishiyaki from Block 1, Heart Mt. He lives in the same hut with me.)

I was going to go fishing, but it seemed like the fish weren't biting today, so I went swimming instead in the Atlantic Ocean. It isn't as wild as the Pacific. Some friends of mine came here last week and caught yellow tail, so I came here to get me one, too, but as I said, the fish weren't biting today.

After that I visited the oldest house in the United States. It was made very strong, and looked very pretty. There was all sorts of old furniture in there. It was all very interesting.

Well, I've still been training very shikari *and* ishsho kemme *[hard and diligently].*

I hope everyone is alright at home. Has Frank come home on furlough yet? I'll be home, (I hope), around the middle of January.

I have to find someplace to eat pretty soon so, goodby for now.

Stanley

P.S. Pa are you still exercising. I still am and I think I'm gaining very slowly.

Camp Blanding, Fla
Nov. 26, 1944

Dear Pa, Ma & Walt,

Well Thanksgiving came and went. I didn't even know it was Thanksgiving until that very day. We had a very big dinner—turkey, fruits, nuts, stuffing, ice cream, cokes—more than I could eat—for once. Everyone was wa bik[k]uri [surprised] at how much I can eat, they say I eat the most in the company. I think I did—anyway I'm about the first in the mess hall and the last one out—and still I'm skinny.

Has Frank come home yet? Sach said he was home on furlough.

Well the army is getting pretty easy now—I'll be home around six more weeks.

Today is Sunday so I guess I'll go work out at the gym. I'm getting a little stronger now. I weigh 135 lbs now. Anata nankashi exercise shi oru [Are you exercising]?

Well I'm hoping everything is alright in Heart MT.

Stanley

Walt, Frank, and a young neighbor, before Frank is shipped overseas.

Everything was not all right in Heart Mountain. His brother Frank was "home" for Thanksgiving, but it was a bleak time as the flag at the administration building flew at half staff and sadness hung over the camp. Ted Fujioka, the first student body president of Heart Mountain High school in 1943, was killed while "on a special mission" in France. One of Ted's closest friends in high school, Pvt. Albert Saijo, was home on leave when the word came. He said that "Ted's whole life had been a special mission . . . to make life better, to make people happier." It is likely that Ted's death added to the constant fears that parents

One Killed, Three Wounded in France
'Ted' Fujioka Dies Performing 'Special Mission'

One Heart Mountain youth was reported killed in action in France this week while three others were reported wounded, according to telegrams received here from the War department by "the next of kin."

Pfc. Teruo "Ted" Fujioka, outstanding student of Heart Mountain high school where he was first president of the student body, was killed Nov. 6 while "on a special mission" according to the War department.

The wounded are:

Pfc. Joe M. Arakaki, son of Taro Arakaki, 27-21-E, who was slightly wounded Nov. 2, in France.

Pfc. George Munetoshi Horiuchi, brother of Mrs. Y. Nakamura, 28-6-A, who was wounded Oct. 16. He had previously won the Purple Heart Cross in Italy.

Pfc. Sam Kageta, son of Mrs. Tsuiko Kageta, 7-14-7, who was slightly wounded Nov. 6, in France.

Ted Fujioka, son of Mr. and Mrs. Shiro Fujioka, 22-14-CD, was 19 on June 12 while fighting in Italy where he was a member of the famous 442nd combat team. After winning his
(Continued on Page 6)

(The following story was written by Pfc. Albert Saijo, who was Pfc. Ted Fujioka's closest high school friend. Private Saijo returned to the center Sunday night on his furlough from Camp Shelby only to learn the next day of the death of his friend. Ed. Note)

By Pfc. Albert Saijo

The War department's telegram to Ted's folks simply said that he had been killed "on a special mission."

His friends here, particularly those with whom he attended school, know that Ted's life was entirely a "special mission". It was a special mission to make life better, to make people happier.

That's the kind of pal Ted Fujioka was.

That's why the American flag flew at half mast at the high school on Monday and that's also the reason that his friend's hearts were sad.

Ted was one soldier who knew what he was fighting for—he told me about it.

It was after he had graduated and we were both working on The Sentinel.

One day after we had covered our runs, Ted said he wanted to talk to me about some-

PFC. 'TED' FUJIOKA

thing. It was spring and there was a tinge of color coming into the McColloughs and the shadows were deepening and the evening shadows shifting.

We walked slowly toward Heart Mountain, beyond the victory gardens, beyond the cemetery with its scraggly plants and up the hillside. We sat down, picked up pebbles and tossed
(Continued on Page 6)

like the Hayamis had for both of their sons.

Camp Blanding, Fla.
Dec. 1944
[No date on letter. Dec. 5 on envelope]

Dear Pa, Ma, & Walt,

Thank you for your letter Pa. I'm glad to hear everyone is OK. Does Frank look any different now? I haven't seen him for about 2 years now.

I guess it was pretty nice at home while he was there, even if it was for only a week.

Well, I am fine, everything is same as usual. Camp Blanding wa tottemo samui desu (is very cold 20°). Next week I go on bivouac too—camp outdoors for 2 wks. Sure is going to be cold.

I'm writing you right now during lunch hour and it's just about time to start work again—I haven't got much to say except that if I don't write for a couple of weeks it's because I'm busy out on bivouac.

I hope everyone is busy and healthy at home. Are you all exercising yet?

Love
Stanley

PS Walt, if the annual ever comes out here's my subscription receipt. Get it for me and save it till I get home.

At last, Frank had come home on furlough and now he was gone. The two brothers had not seen each other for such a long time. Sach was not at home, either. She was in New York. They were all a long way from each other with no way of knowing when they would all be together again.

Being separated from family during the holidays is difficult even in peacetime, but it had to be especially lonely for young soldiers like Stanley. A relatively new song, "White Christmas," held special meaning for soldiers who were far from home. Wyoming was not truly home, but it was the place that soldiers, like Stan, surely thought of when they heard crooner Bing Crosby singing the lyrics . . . "I'm dreaming of a White Christmas, just like the ones I used to know . . . "

Although camping out during basic training was tough going, somewhere along the way, Stan managed to find and send a Christmas card home to thank the family for the treats they had sent to him for the holidays. He wrote this on the back of the card . . .

Dec 18, 1944

Dear Folks,

Thanks a lot for the nuts. Sure get hungry out here on bivouac. I'm camping out for the past week and will be camping out for the next week, too. I get to go back to Camp Blanding in time for Christmas.

I wanted to get you folks X-mas presents, but I couldn't get around to it as I am out here camping. But when I come home very shortly I will try to bring some things home (if I have enough money). Anyway I'll be sure and get you your "smokes" Pop.

Sach says Frank was in New York the other day. I guess he will go across soon. Hope he takes good care of himself.

Merry X-mas & Happy New Year.
Stanley

When he wrote this card Stanley had no way of knowing what a big surprise Christmas 1944 would bring for the Hayami family in Wyoming. Just weeks earlier Stanley told them that he would not get home before late January. Now, suddenly, his basic training ended! Stanley was able to get to Heart Mountain in time for Christmas! His name is listed in the December 30th issue of the newspaper. He was one of 21 soldiers on leave for the holiday. On the front page, in bold type, it says that there are now 567 soldiers serving their country from Heart Mountain.

Stanley does not write about his feelings in returning to Heart Mountain, wearing the same uniform as the soldiers standing guard at the entry of this bleak, wind-swept city of barracks. He returned to live inside a prison camp, surrounded with barbed wire, that his parents and brother were not free to leave. The hypocrisy was apparent.

Among the soldiers on leave was Roy Kawamoto, who would be sent overseas with Stan. In the window of the Hayami barrack there was a small flag with two blue stars bordered with red, signifying that two members of the family

Visitors

SERVICEMEN—Pvt. Tom Yoshikai, Pvt. Mas Nishimoto, Pvt. Shigeo Fujii, Pvt. Toshibumi Hanada, Pvt. Stanley Hayami, Pvt. Takeshi Ishizaki, Pvt. Frank Kogata, Pvt. Eddie Kawakami, Pvt. Roy Kawamoto, Pvt. Isao Kudow, Pvt. Al Mitsunaga, Pvt. Tamotsu Nishimura, Pvt. Kaoru Nishida, Pvt. Kazuo Umemoto, Pvt. Ken Teramura, Pvt. Thomas Okumura, Pvt. Frank Sato, Pvt. Tadashi Sato, Pvt. Seichi Shimizu, Pvt. Joe Umemoto, Fort Lewis, Wash.; Toshio Mihara, Italy.

CIVILIANS — Hank Takeda, Takeichi Takeda, Kiwa Koga, Kiku Seiyama, Yaeko Sumii, Denver; Clarence Nishizu, Rikio Sato, Caldwell, Ida.; Haruo Uyeda, Isao Yuge, Idaho Falls, Ida.; Harry H. Fujii, Robert Kuwahara, George Mitsunaga, Miyoko Miyauchi, Mary Nakashima, Toyo Oka, Chicago, Ill.; Kazuko Terada, Oskaloosa, Ia.; Larry Shimada, Kansas City, Kan.; Fumio Hangai, George Iwanaga, Kenji Taniguchi, Minneapolis, were in military service.

Like Stan's family, the Kawamotos had two sons of draft age. But Dave Kawamoto, the older brother, refused to enter the service while his family remained incarcerated. In 1941 when World War II began, Dave was about to graduate from San Jose College. He tried to enlist at once, but the army rejected him along with thousands of other Nisei. Dave was so bitter at being labeled an enemy alien, that when the draft was applied to Nisei, he refused to answer the draft on constitutional grounds. He was imprisoned with other resisters in Leavenworth, a Federal prison in Kansas.

Such decisions not only divided the community, they also split some families apart. However, the Kawamotos felt that their sons were entitled to make their own decisions. They were proud of both brothers, who remained good friends in spite of their differences of opinion over the way to serve their country and the Constitution.

Stanley's furlough photo with his parents and Walt, Christmas 1944.

Like other visiting GIs, Stanley posed proudly for his photo in uniform with his family. Happy as they were to have Stanley with them, it had to be a sad and frightening time for the Hayamis. They had one son already headed overseas and now, another would follow in no time at all. Walt recalls that his parents didn't express any of their fears to him, although he knew they were apprehensive about Stanley going. They were supportive of him, Walt explained . . .

I think Stan saw both sides of the issue and he made a conscious choice. Yes, he did. He made his own decision. He only had six weeks of basic training and then they sent him over. I guess the Army was desperate for replacements. I was proud that he was going.

Walter Hayami, interview with author, Nov. 4, 2004

The army urgently needed to replace the terrible losses of the invasion of Europe and especially those of the 442nd RCT, which had lost many men in Italy and the mountains of France. It is true, Stan's basic training was cut short, but not as short as Walter recalled more than sixty years later. In fact, Stan writes on Nov. 1 that he is starting the eighth week of training. Basic training was 17 weeks. Stan had less than 15 full weeks.

Insignia of the 442nd RCT

An editorial in the same December 30th newspaper announces that the Nikkei are free to return to California. That news was greeted with mixed emotions. Few people had homes or businesses to which they could return. Most took a wait-and-see attitude toward returning, while many were determined to go to the Midwest or East. Time would tell if they would be welcome in California. Stan had no options. He was about to go further from home than ever.

Jan. 1, 1945

American ✚ Red Cross
CANTEEN
LAMBERT FIELD :: ST. LOUIS, MO.

Dear Me, Pa, Walt
    Happy New Year — ima wa
su koshi 12 oclock no past desu.
    Tadao wo telephone shi moshite
Tadao ga mini kimashita! Na ga ku
"talk." shi moshita— "lucky" datta mitta— m.
    Stanley Yoshida wo Casper de me moshita.
mitta "lucky" datta ne.
        nan demo "thank you" oishi mono
wo tabete "Merry X-mas" datta.
    matta Happy New Year

Kunio

1945

Stanley's next letter is dated January 1, 1945. In fact, there are two letters dated January 1, 1945 and only one envelope, so they may have been mailed together. One is on American Red Cross stationery from Lambert Field in St. Louis, Mo. It says . . .

Jan. 1, 1945

Dear Ma, Pa, Walt

Happy New Year—ima wa sukoshi *12 oclock* no *past* desu *[it is a little past 12:00]. Tadao* wo *telephone* shimashite *Tadao* ga mini kimashita *[I telephoned Tadao [Takano], and Tadao came to see me]!* Nagaku *"talk"* shimashita *[We talked for a long time]. "Lucky"* datta mitta no *[I was lucky we got to see each other].*

Stanley Yoshida wo *Casper* de mimashita. Matta *"lucky"* datta ne *[Saw Stanley Yoshida in Casper (Wyo.). Again I was lucky].*

Nan demo "thank you" oishi mono wo tabete *"Merry X-mas"* datta *[Thank you for everything. I had good things to eat and it was a merry X-mas].*

Matta (again) Happy New Year

Kunio

Written almost entirely in Japanese, this is the one and only letter Stanley signed in *Romaji* with his Japanese name, *Kunio.*

Stan was *en route* to the European theater of operations on New Year's Eve in December 1944. The first leg of the trip brought him to St. Louis, where his old school friend Tadao Takano was living. Tad vividly recalls that New Year's eve . . .

I was a houseboy at a private residence while attending Washington University in St. Louis. I don't know how he got my number but I was in tears . . . I wanted to see him and my people were going out to a New Year's party. I told them what was happening and that Stan

Stan's good friend, Tad.

143

wanted me to come out to Lambert Field and they said to go ahead. So I took a streetcar down to the Chase Hotel and from there I took the bus. But when I got there I couldn't find anything. Lambert Field was pretty much in a blackout situation and I recall wandering about between all manner of aircraft looking for his group, restricted to quarters, after the first leg of the journey from Camp Shelby.

Finally I decided this is hopeless, so I caught the shuttle bus and an officer sat down next to me. He said are you looking for someone? I said yes and I mentioned Stanley's name and he said well at the next stop you get off and I think you'll find him there . . . So I did that and there was a guard outside and they wouldn't let me go in, but he went in and got Stanley. We talked outside for about fifteen minutes or so. I recall little of the cold outdoor conversation—but for one thing . . . he told me that he had only undergone very limited training but the situation in Europe was rather dire what with the Battle of the Bulge aftermath and the need for replacements.

Tadao Takano interview with author, April 2005

Tad insists that Stan was not complaining. But maybe Stan should have. As he spoke about that time, Tad kept returning to the fact that Stan's outfit had so little training; while he remembered his own unit having more than twice that much training and he still felt inadequate.

Tad is not alone in feeling that all too many Nisei soldiers had been given impossible tasks and suffered grievous losses as a result. More than one veteran of the 442nd, including Tad, concluded that too many Nisei troops were sacrificed as "cannon fodder." Some felt that their commanding officers considered them expendable.

But the overriding sentiment of those who served was belief that they had to show their loyalty as Americans. A young Hawaiian volunteer, Daniel Inouye, recalled that when he was leaving for the service his father told him, "America has been good to us . . . It has given you and your sisters and brothers education. We all love this country. Whatever you do, do not dishonor your country. Remember: Never dishonor your family. And if you must give your life, do so with honor."

Nikkei families on the mainland shared this cultural belief, to bring no shame to one's family. Among those living inside of WRA barbed wire prison camps there were many who felt a deep bitterness and shame of being incarcerated. No matter how innocent, they suffered a sense of embarrassment and anger that others might think they had done something wrong.

For many Nisei soldiers these feelings translated into a need to prove something more than other units fighting in Europe. From the desert sands of North Africa, to the beaches of Salerno, Anzio, and on to Rome, and the south of France, the valor and sacrifices of Japanese American troops began to appear in news.

In June of 1944, the 100th Infantry Battalion, from Hawaii became an integral part of the 442nd RCT. Together they began to make history as the most decorated fighting unit of its size in U.S. Army. Their courage as well as the horrific demands made of the Nisei troops are perhaps best illustrated with an event that happened in late October of 1944 in the Battle for the Lost Battalion, when the 442nd proved its valor, but was reduced to half its original force.

For six days of bloody combat, the Nisei soldiers were ordered to rescue more than 200 soldiers of the 1st Battalion, 141st Infantry Regiment, 36th "Texas" Infantry Division, who were trapped behind enemy lines in the Vosges Mountains, in France. The Nisei troops were sent out to do what others had failed to do. They courageously made their way over steep hills, ravines, and through German minefields to reach the stranded battalion. But the price was staggering. In rescuing so many, the Nisei lost 216 men killed in action and more than 856 men wounded. Platoons that started out with 32 men were reduced to 11 or fewer. Squads of 15 men returned with 3 or 4 soldiers. By mid-November the 442nd RCT was decimated.

Long after these events, many say that their sacrifices made all the difference in the way the Nisei and future generations of Japanese Americans would be accepted. It was a brutal price that they paid, for rights that they should never have lost.

During that winter of 1944–45, the entire U.S. Army in Europe desperately needed replacements, not just for the Nisei who had fallen in the battle for the Lost Battalion, but on the bloody beaches of Normandy, in the Battle of the Hurtgen Forest, and the deadly Battle of the Bulge, when the Americans suffered an estimated 76,000 casualties in December 1944 and January 1945.

In the face of such losses replacements were rushed to Europe. Stanley Hayami was one of those being sent to fill the ranks.

He was one of the 1,214 replacements, mostly draftees from the mainland, who would be serving side by side with the survivors of historic battles. Many were boys like Stan, who had just finished high school. Most of the "old-timers" were young Hawaiian Nisei, soldiers just barely in their 20s, who had been recruited in 1943.

More than 6 decades have passed, but for Tad Takano the memory of his visit with his good friend Stanley is still vivid. It was a cold New Year's Eve when the world would ring out 1944 and welcome 1945.

Tad was still bothered by these memories. His voice broke as he spoke . . .

> It was criminal you know! I was in the army and in 17 weeks of basic training we weren't really ready. I don't know why they were doing that . . . and they were flying them! All transportation was by train in those days, but they flew them up to St. Louis and then I guess to the east coast for shipping them overseas . . . they needed replacements!
>
> *Tadao Takano interview with author, April 2005*

More than 60 years later Tad continued to compare himself with his good friend, Stanley. He paused and then added . . .

> So much more to say, but Stanley can be summed up as being very sweet. He was optimistic . . .I wasn't . . .He had plans for the future, I never even thought about the future.

Stanley's next letter, dated January 1st, was not from St. Louis. Stan had flown from St. Louis to Ft. Meade, a base in Maryland, and then on to somewhere on the East Coast, where he would board a troopship to Europe. Where they sailed from was a military secret.

Dear Folks,

I am no longer at Ft. Meade, but I am still somewhere on the east coast— the exact place I can't say.

I'm O.K. and feeling fine, I hope you are too.

Tell me, have you been getting my $7.50 war bonds? I have increased the amount of my bonds to the $18.75 bond. The reason I did this is because I am going to get 20% overseas pay which in my case is $10 more. I now get $60 per month.

I am still going to send $20 home every month. I want you to keep 10 bucks for yourself and save ten for me. If you need it, you may use all of it.

This is the way I'm going to distribute my pay.

$ 18.75 BONDS

$ 6.50 INSURANCE

$ 20.00 SENDING HOME

Total $45.25

Remainder $14.75 for me to spend. This should be enough as I don't think I'll need much money overseas. Besides I may lose my money if I'm carrying it around over there.

This letter is reminiscent of Stan's "budget" in his diary entry of March 8, 1943 and an earlier letter of September 17, 1944. Stan is something of an accountant. He obviously likes knowing what he has and how it is to be spent. In the earlier letters he seems most interested in proving his independence. Now he steps up to a new level of responsibility by providing for his parents and their needs before he leaves, knowing he might be gone forever.

Stan's $60 a month pay represented a great deal to him. In 1945 it was not a huge sum, but it was significant, especially to Nikkei families that had lost so much when they were incarcerated. Inside the camps, professionals such as doctors were paid $19 a month; the majority of workers earned only $12–$16 a month. Teenagers generally had part-time jobs that paid $8 a month. With such limited salaries, those who came into the camps with savings often used up their money to cover their expenses.

The money Stan sent home would be important to the family as they looked ahead to returning to California. The Hayamis were more fortunate than most. They had property to return to. Their nursery business was in bad shape, but they had a home. Stan was telling them to save some for him, but the rest was for them. Taking care of one's elders was a cultural tradition.

More than a month passed before the Hayamis heard from Stanley again. That was not surprising since troop convoys sailing from the East Coast of the United States to Europe took close to a month to cross the Atlantic. The crossings were fraught with danger. American ships often went south where they were more easily protected by land-based anti-submarine air patrols. They would also zigzag across the ocean to avoid being easy targets for German U-boats that sank whatever supply and troopships they could find. Troopships could take as long as 28 days to cross the ocean. Many GIs recall being seasick for a good part of the journey.

The first mail the Hayamis received came in the form of V-mail, a special kind of war-time letter and envelope all-in-one, that was photographed onto 16mm film, miniaturized, and shipped by plane. The film was then printed at a center nearest the recipient's home. Ultimately, the V-mail delivered was about a quarter the size of the original letter. V-mail was faster, allowing a letter to get to GIs or home in 12 days or less, while regular mail might take as long as six weeks by ship.

Stan's V-mail is postmarked stateside on Feb 12, 1945 . . .

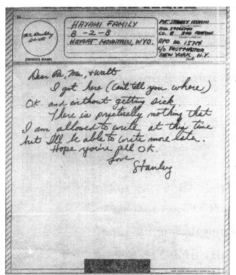

Stan's first V-mail home.

Dear Pa, Ma, & Walt,

I got here (I can't tell you where) O.K. and without getting sick.

There is practically nothing that I am allowed to write at this time but I'll be able to write more later.

Hope you're all O.K.

Love
Stanley

This brief message was Stan's first letter from Europe. The next newsy letter below probably took a lot longer to reach home.

The stamp on the left shows that the letter was examined. The stamp on the right shows the kinds of planes used to fly air mail letters.

Somewhere in France
Feb 7, 1945

Dear Pa, Ma, & Walt,

Well here I am in France. I don't feel like I'm in France though.

I still feel like I am in the U.S. There a difference though—the houses look older; some crumbled by the bombs. The people seem very poor (of course, I have seen only the lower classes.) They wear clothes that are worn and patched and faded. We were having "chow" near the railroad tracks, and being a wasteful people, we threw some of the food we didn't feel like eating on the ground. Pretty soon some old Frenchmen came by and picked up the scraps of bread and baloney. One of them saw me watching and so he pointed at the Baloney and said "woof woof". I guess he had a little pride and wanted me to think that he was picking it up to feed to his dog, but I don't think poor Frenchmen like him spend a great deal of their time looking for scraps just so they can feed it to their dogs.

Food shortages in Europe 1945 were widespread. In France some of the male population was taken to Germany as slave labor. This left the farms without the normal labor force. The German occupiers hadn't hesitated to take the best food for their troops (as well as any fine art and other valuables they wanted) leaving the civilian population with little in the way of basics. In addition, Allied bombers did whatever they could to knock out railways and trucking on roads across Europe. All of this explains why Frenchmen, like the one in Stan's letter, were reduced to taking scraps of food wherever they could find them.

The kids are really pests. We'd be marching along and they come running up and tag along. They're skinny and dirty and I feel kindda sorry for them. They ask for "cigarette". "kindy" (candy), "goom" (gum). But boy, if you give one of them a piece of candy or something a whole crowd of them come running up—they yank at your coat, and hang onto your cartridge belt, and look into your pockets. 'Nother thing about those kids they wear short pants like in our country, but also wear short dresses over it!

I still don't know where I'm going to end up, but I guess I'll know soon.

Has Frank written yet? I guess I'll catch up with him pretty soon.

Pa, have you decided to return to California? Boy I guess it'll be a long time before I get home to California.

Well keep healthy—exercise and get plenty of fresh air. Ma, Pa, & Walt please write when you can.

Love,
Stanley

This is the first of several letters in which Stanley asks about the family's possible return to California. Before December of 1944, Nikkei who had signed loyalty papers could go "outside" of the camps to work or go to college, but they were not free to return to the West Coast. Now, at last, the ban was lifted. The government not only knew there was no threat of a Japanese attack on the West Coast, they also feared that prohibiting the return of the Nikkei might be found unconstitutional in the courts. Nevertheless, the news that they could legally return to California was followed with a storm of hatred in cities, especially on the West Coast.

Newspaper columnists threatened there would be bloodshed if the Nikkei returned and indeed, some who returned early were subjected to drive-by shootings and threats. Inside the camps there was a reluctance to return to such racist hostility. Few had money in the bank for starting over or homes to live in. For many there was little choice but to stay in the camps and wait. The Hayami's had not yet decided what they would do.

In mid-February Frank wrote home about a wonderful surprise . . .

Feb 15
Southern France

Hello Everybody-

How are all of you. Hope the cold isn't getting you down. Bet it's pretty cold there. Wear more clothes to bed like I do and stay warm.

Well anyway, today, just by chance I happened to see Stanley. I was going someplace, but we stopped by this place, and there he was, eating chow so I hopped out of my jeep and visited with him all afternoon.

He's looking very fine—and sure has gained much weight since I saw him back in Heart Mountain—nice and husky now. Big hands and big body. And still smiling his nice big smile. He was eating an extra marmalade sandwich when I saw him. Man, he sure eats now. I sure am gaining weight. I try to cut down weight by not eating breakfast, but that doesn't help. He could use some more weight.

He gave me some candy & cigarettes. He's kind of dirty because he hasn't washed in a long tine. It's hard to wash up over here-but so far it's o.k. because it's not too warm.

Say, did my guitar and ukulele get to you from Camp Shelby? Stanley said that only the box got home.

By the way, when are you going to write to me mama san & papa san? No shame. The letters from you are not censored. But since coming over, I haven't received one letter from you. What's the matter. Maybe, it's slow delivery over here.

Anyway Stanley's fine. Wasn't so sick at all he says. Just hungry. Some of the boys were green in the face, he says. While we're here in Southern France don't worry about us for we're O.K. Everything's nice and peaceful here.

I guess Stanley will write to you soon-as soon as he settles down. I'll write more later. Til then, this is your son-

au Revoir—
Frank

Feb 17, 1945
Southern France

Dear Folks—

Visited Stanley yesterday before he was moved away to his assigned company. Got down there just as he had finished eating—and there he was—a big lanky guy with a towel around his neck and his mess kit in his hand. Army life seems to have done him some good—or maybe it was the weight lifting.

Took a camera down with me and took some pictures of him since this will probably be the last time I'll be <u>able</u> to see him—unless we get our rest periods at the same time—which I doubt. Anyway, he and I are in different companies—many miles apart. Will send you some of those pictures if they turn out O.K. Am sending a picture that someone took of me and two other fellows. As you can see I'm still the same. No change-except my hair which is standing straight up.

Met Mr. Sunahara who used to live in our block—you know, the man with four kids—anyway, he, Stanley, and I took a picture together and will send you some. Also met the brother of the kid who used to pal around with Tomo. Lotsa Heart Mountain Boys—some I didn't know—some I knew— Omar Kaohatsu, Shig Marumoto, and a host of others.

Stanley was assigned to "E" Company, so now his address is.
PVT. Stanley _____, _____

E Co, 2nd BN. 442 RG

APO 758

C/O P.M., New York, NY

He'll probably write to you right away with his address but I'm sure this is right. Be sure to write to him since he says he hasn't had a letter from you since leaving the states.

Say if you've got a 120 or a 620 camera around your house, I'd sure like to have it if you can spare it/ I can buy beau???? (that's French for lots) films here—costs quite a bit but it's the best souvenir.

Tonight, I'm on duty from Midnight to 9AM—it's 3 AM now . . . and the radio's getting noisy again—dots and dashes. So I'll say Bon Nuit (good nite)

Your loving son,

Frank

Frank's education as an electrical engineer helped him get a better job than most foot soldiers. He was a radio operator, decoding messages at 442nd Headquarters. Now that he found Stan, he made it his business to stay in touch whenever he could.

Stan didn't write home "right away," as Frank put it. His Company E, 2nd Battalion was on the move and he didn't get around to writing about their meeting for weeks. His letter tells how thrilled he was to see his older brother for the first time since Frank left for New York. But their reunion was brief. Stan's company covered a lot of territory in this short time. The end of Stan's next letter reveals just how close he is now to the horrors of the front lines.

[Note the date on the letter below: Stan seems to have lost track of the dates— the envelope is postmarked Feb 27th . . . there was no 30th of February, even in 1945 . . .]

Somewhere in France
Feb. 30, 1945

Well, I finally caught up with Frank. The first day I joined the 442 I met him. Frank happened to come down to the place I was to take a shower and I came walking out of the mess and by golly I thought I saw a familiar face—

well God dammit! It was Frank! I guess it was the first time I saw him in 2 yrs., but he hasn't changed at all. I was plenty glad to see him! We went up where I was staying and talked for about 2 hrs. I guess Frank didn't take a shower. Next day Frank came to see me again and we took some pictures together. Jimmy Sunahara came [the] same time as me; and Frank, Jimmy and I had our picture taken together. Frank says he has a swell job over here as radio operator.

Well since I last wrote, I've been to Paris and Marseilles. I didn't get too good a look at Paris as I only saw it from the back of a truck, but what I did see looked pretty good. Looks like almost any big town back home. Streets are pretty wide and clean and the shops look expensive.

For a person like Stan who dreamed of traveling it must have been frustrating to only get a peek of Paris from the back of a truck! Still he liked what he saw, even though it was a tough, uncomfortable ride. They were really jammed inside with a squad of 12 to 15 guys with all their gear packed into the back of these trucks.

After days on the road or up in the mountains, getting a shower was a luxury. The shower facilities in the base camp must have reminded Stan of Wyoming, only more crowded. This exchange from an official journal gives us a small view of how it must have been: "How many men will be coming to take shower?" a radioman asked. The answer was "about 100 per hour." "That's too much," he was told. "Hold it down. Try 4-minutes per man." There was no wood to heat the water, only some coal.

Stan's letter continues . . .

Right now I'm up front here, living on top of a mountain. The Jerries are on the next mountain. It's nice and warm up here, get enough to eat, don't do much, and the Germans aren't giving us too much trouble (not now, anyway)

All in all it's pretty good up here and I guess I would just about forget the war if it wasn't for the artillery lobbing shells over us and if I couldn't see the dead Jerries lying round below. (They were killed before I got here when they tried to attack.) I didn't feel so good when I first saw the dead Jerries, but no one pays much attention to them when we go working around them—they're just part of the landscape now. So the dead ones don't bother me anymore— they say it's the live ones I should worry about.

Well have you decided to go home to California, Pa?

How's that rugged brudder Wally doing? You studying for a change? Guess you ain't. How's Tome & George and the rest?

Mama, you madda gakko ni ikkimasu *(you still going to school)?*

Papa madda shogi asubioru no *(are you still playing* **shogi***)?*

Well that's about all for now—please write often. I haven't received any letters yet—Frank only got one so far and he's been here 2 mts.

Love
Stanley

Stanley and the soldiers of the 2nd and 3rd Battalion were stationed in defensive positions in the Maritime Alps above the French Riviera that winter. They moved from one outpost to the next trudging through snowy slopes and living in dry dugouts that were colder than the barracks Stan had left at Heart Mountain. Their supplies of canned meat and other items came by mule train because the trails were too steep and winding for army trucks.

Stanley uses the derogatory slang word "Jerries" to describe German soldiers. According to legend, in W.W. I, German soldiers wore helmets in battle that looked like old-fashioned chamber pots. These were also known as jeroboams, so the word was shortened to "Jerries."

Although serving in Southern France at this time was considered more like garrison duty, there were sniper attacks, surprise assaults, and minefields that took the lives of GIs. Enemy infiltrators, "line crossers," as they called them, were a constant problem as they tried to blend in with the troops and gather information. The enemy was never far away.

Now, for the first time, Stan is living face-to-face with the terrifying sound of artillery shells exploding, the ever-present threat of being wounded or worse, and the haunting sight of dead soldiers. For Stanley and his buddies, the bloody horrors of war are no longer something imagined. They are living with the ugly reality of the carnage; the sights, sounds, and sickening smells of the battlefield. Hard experience taught Stan not to worry about dead Germans, only live ones. Today it was them—tomorrow it could be him.

Stan's next letter on March 4th must have caused alarm when it arrived on American Red Cross stationery just a few days later. In fact, Stanley is in the hospital!

Dear Pa, Ma, Walt,

Well I was up in the mountains like I told you when I got "it" and got stuck in this hospital.

But don't worry, it wasn't bullets that put me in here, it was Measles! (I thought I had measles before) So right now I'm in bed in a very modern and beautiful French hospital. The hospital is in a very famous French town and from my bed I can look out and get a very good view of it. The food is very good and I am served in bed! I feel very good and all I have to do is sit or lie down and read, But I'd rather be back up in the mountains!

Up front in the mountains, I was just getting used to it. Like I told you it wasn't very dangerous and I was learning a lot from the old timers. My sergeant is a very young kid yet, only 20, but he is very wise and experienced in warfare—He has the D.S.C. and French Croix de Guerre—also Purple Heart with cluster!

I haven't seen Frank . . . but I've written to him.

Well how goes Heart Mountain? Getting warmer? Sis you get my last letter? I dated my last letter wrong- I thought it was the 30th of Feb when it really was only the 25th. Tell me how long it takes to get [this] home.

I hope everyone is O.K.

Love Stanley

We know from the rare cluster of medals Stan mentions in his letter, that the sergeant he was writing about had to be Tsuneo Takemoto, one of the few survivors of the Lost Battalion rescue. Lawson Sakai, a veteran of the 442nd remembers Takemoto as "the most fearless leader in the war, leading his whole company in an attack, even though he was just the third platoon sergeant."

From his description we know Stan was also impressed by all the awards his sergeant had won. But Stan was not in France long before Sergeant Takemoto was seriously wounded and shipped back home. A young officer, 2nd Lt. Dan Inouye became the third platoon commander and took over the leadership of Stan's platoon, Company E, 2nd Battalion, of the 442nd RCT.

Newly arrived soldiers, like Stan, were not always befriended by battle-weary GIs who were afraid to get too close to replacements. "Old-timers" had lived through the heartbreak of seeing too many good friends die or bloodied in combat. For many, the best way to protect against repeating such painful losses was to avoid anyone new.

Stan's letters show that he often saw guys from home and his brother . . .

Southern France
March 19, 1945

Dear Ma, Pa, & Walt,

Well I've gotten out of the hospital. No more measles.

I've seen Frank 4 or 5 times since I last wrote. I also saw Willie . . . Frank, me, & Willie had our pictures taken together. That's the first I time I saw Willie in a long time too (about two years) but he looks about the same. Only difference is he has a tooth missing and his eyes looked tired.

Frank has been very nice to me- he even came to see me when I was in the hospital.

Thanks you all very much for the letters I had a lot of fun reading them. Don't worry about sending me things. I'll ask if I need anything. Right now I don't need anything. I get plenty of candy, gum, cigarettes and etc. either free or for a small sum. I always give my cigarettes and beer away 'cuz I still don't smoke or drink—yet. Dare demo wa boku ni uimasu *(Everyone says to me),* Stanley one big battle and you'll change! *"Nervous"* natte nanika wo noman to dame *(You will get nervous and you must drink something). I saw Murata too.* Murata **wa** *"last year"* **ni kitta toki 442 wa hidoi kenka ni h[a]iteta no** *(When Murata came last year the 442 was in a very big battle. Murata* wa boku ni uimasu "senso wa tottemo kuwai desu" *(Murata tells me "war is very scary").*

I also saw Moe Yonemura. I didn't get a chance to talk to him though.

Remember David Ito? He got a bronze star medal the other day.

Remember Yo and Mas Tsuruda that lived near us in Pomona? Well their brother is in my company and he won a silver star!

Mas Kadota is in my own company! Looks darker that's all, if that's possible.

*I haven't got **senbei** (Japanese rice crackers) and nuts yet, but I guess packages take longer than air mail letter (15 days)*

How are you folks at home? Frank says you may go home to California about May. How are your false teeth Pa? You oughta have a lot of fun if you go back to Calif. Eh, Walt. I'd sure like to be going home with you. Frank, too.

Well please don't worry about me. I'm having fun (right now at least) Weather's fine, guys are swell, get plenty to eat, even see movies now and then—so it's pretty good, only trouble is there's a war on yet, and I'm not at home. Well take care of yourselves ma, pa, & Walt.

Love,

Stanley

P.S. Did Frank send any pics of us home yet? Here's one of me waiting in line to wash my mess gear. Frank took the picture.

Although there was some fighting in France, this brief interlude is what the men called the "Champagne Campaign." It was a relatively peaceful time for new recruits, like Stan, to fit in with the experienced GIs who would be their brothers in arms. Through intensive training and classes they began to become a unit. They were sent out on night patrols, to deactivate mines and booby traps, and to attend "Mule School," learning how to get the mule trains moving.

Untried soldiers like Stan were in awe at the "old-timers," soldiers who were themselves boys of 20 and 21. They were in the south of France, not far from Nice, Cannes, Antibes, and Monaco on the French Riviera where an abundance of wine and women entertained battle-weary soldiers as well as the new replacements. French families welcomed the soldiers into their homes and children followed the GIs begging for candy and chewing gum. It was a fair weather time to soak up some fun, to hope that the rumors of a German

Frank, Stan, and Cousin Willie in France, 1945

surrender were true.

In early March the Nisei soldiers began to hear rumors that the 442nd would soon be on the move again. Their destination was a military secret, but there was little doubt that the 442nd was now back to fighting strength and they would soon be in combat. During that time soldiers of the 522nd Field Artillery Battalion of the 442nd were sent north to fight with the 7th Army in their efforts to push into Germany. The others waited for orders.

General Mark Clark, the commanding general of the 15th Army Group, made up mainly of the US Fifth Army and the British Eighth Army, had been preparing for a major offensive to claim Northern Italy from the Germans.

"Old-timers" of the 442nd had been in Italy before. They left here just eight months earlier to serve in France. All winter and fall the Germans had worked at fortifying their fighting positions, constructing gun pits and trenches all along the Italian Apennine Mountains. This was the Germans' last stronghold, the so-called Gothic Line, designed to keep the Allies from breaking through the Po Valley to Austria and Germany.

General Clark had requested the 100th/442nd to lead the assault from the west. He knew these men and their courageous record. He believed the 100th/442nd could accomplish what others had failed to do. So far they had won every battle they had ever been assigned to fight. They seemed to be invincible. General Clark planned a pincer attack across the whole width of Northern Italy. On the Eastern coast the British Commandos and the British Eighth Army would make their assault on that side of the Gothic Line. Meanwhile the American Fifth Army and the men of the 100th/442nd were to spearhead the attack on the west side. Clark's strategy was to surprise the enemy and take them with overwhelming force.

Their objective was to break through the fortifications and push the Germans out of Italy to their final defeat. For years the Germans had fought their battles away from their homeland, waging war on foreign soil. Italy was no exception. All that winter the Germans had used slave labor to construct more than 2,000 machine gun nests and lookout sites that could destroy any Allied attempt to break through the Gothic Line. German troops were now well entrenched in fortifications dug out of solid rock and reinforced with concrete. They also occupied the many small villages nestled in the formidable rocky terrain of the Apennine Mountains.

On March 22nd the rumors turned to reality. The men of the 442nd RCT had their orders. They moved out of the staging area near Antibes, France by motor convoy. They arrived at the port in Marseilles and at 2:30 AM Stanley was among those who were loaded with their equipment onto Landing Ship Tanks (LSTs). These ships were as long as 328 feet and could carry 2100 tons including trucks and tanks. Their bow doors opened, like a closet for a giant, and vehicles rode in or out on a ramp. They left the following afternoon at 4 PM. They were at sea on the 24th and the weather was clear.

A puzzling note in the 442's official narrative mentions that the men pounded their spoons on silver quarters on the ship railing. Jimmy Yamashita of Company I recalled, "There was little to do physically on such a ship. Usually a craps game would begin. To pass the time away many men hammered silver coins into rings that they could send home to someone they loved. They used a silver half dollar or quarter that was pounded and bent with a spoon or the heel of a shoe on the ship's railing. The endless tap-tap-tapping annoyed more than one skipper."

On one LST, some of the GIs were reading or enjoying the sun, when they were suddenly startled by an alarming call—"Torpedo on the portside!" someone called. Many remember hitting the deck in alarm, others just froze and waited in silence. It was their lucky day! The torpedo missed! They thanked their lucky stars and some began pounding their silver coins again as if nothing had happened.

On the 25th of March the LST's arrived at Livorno, Italy. The port was so littered with sunken ships that the troops used the wrecked hulls as stepping-stones. Now on Italian soil, the GIs traveled by truck convoy to their base camp near San Martino, about 40 miles north. On the way they surely passed by the medieval city of Pisa. Stanley never mentions seeing the famous Leaning Tower of Pisa, a sight he would have been thrilled to see in other times. But this was no sightseeing trip.

At the foot of the soaring granite cliffs of the Apennine Mountains that rose almost directly from the Ligurian Sea, the Nisei soldiers readied for their attack. Their days were filled with endless training classes and drills. They continued practicing moving mule trains with supplies, because the narrow mountain trails again made it impossible to move supplies by truck. Briefings prepared the troops for mines and other tactical problems. In their limited free time, those who wanted showers were taken by truck to the shower area. Clean clothes, hot

We take rations up to where we are by mule.

Mountains are plenty steep when we started. I was leading the mule, But by the time I reached the top.

Here's me when I landed over here

But this was me before I got the measles

AMERICAN RED CROSS

FORM 539 A

food, and showers were luxuries. There wasn't much to look forward to except the mail and the hope that they would be lucky enough to get home alive someday.

They were given not just standard "C" rations, but beer, peanuts, cigarettes (13 per man), and sometimes a Coca-Cola (one per man). In the evenings there were films that allowed some escape and entertainment. Their days were filled with two-hour hikes to ready them for the rigorous days ahead. There were squad and platoon exercises and a nervous certainty that they would soon be in battle.

Stan wrote his next letter the day after he arrived in Italy. Note his return address below. He doesn't even say he is in Italy. His location is a military secret.

Somewhere in E.T.O. [European Theater of Operations] March 26, 1945

Stan held onto his sense of humor.

Dear Pa, Ma, & Walt,

Well How de doody! I'm still in plenty good health—yet. Weather is fine—except it keeps on raining.

It's pretty warm here Ma, but I guess that sweater you knit me will come in handy at nite. Please send it. Its still cold at nite.

I saw Frank again. He gave me one of his pocketknives, which I needed.

I got a couple letters from you, Pa & Ma a couple days ago and another from Wally today—V-mail. Thanks a lot every one!

It's starting to rain again, I just put my laundry (long underwear, handker-

chiefs) inside. The other nite I saw a couple of good pictures. "Cover Girl" and "Up In Arms" Sure was good.

Well, there isn't much else. Please tell me all about when you go back to California.

*Love
Stanley*

April 1st had always been a time for silly April Fool's tricks. But there was little to joke about on the first of April 1945, a warm, rainy Easter Sunday. Two years earlier, Stanley wrote in his diary about becoming a Christian on Easter Sunday in Heart Mountain. Now here he was in Italy, at services conducted by army chaplains, praying with other young men as they prepared for what would be his "baptism of fire," his first real battle. In his next letter he writes vaguely about where he is. Whatever fears he had, he did not share them with his family.

*April 2, 1945
Somewhere in Italy*

Dear Ma, Pa, & Walt,

Well, doggone, here I am in Italy now! After studying all that French, I gotta learn Italian now! Fooey!

Yesterday was Easter and I went to the services. Reminded me of all the other Easters I've had. Guess I'll remember this one for a long time.

Got two more letters from you and you Pa & Ma. Thanks. Sure makes me feel good to get a letter.

I can't write too much tonite —cuz the candle is burning low.

Make that sweater V neck Ma.

Hope your false teeth fit good Pa.

How goes school Walt?

*'Nuff for now
Stanley*

P.S. Don't worry about me. Italy is a nice place—weather like California.

Ever the optimist, Stanley tells the family not to worry; yet those who were there knew the 442nd was about to embark on a campaign that would demand grave sacrifices. Stan wrote home on the eve of this major offensive. But for many days we have no letters from Stanley telling us in his own words what he was experiencing. To fill in the gaps, we have relied on other sources, such as official 442nd narratives in the Journals of Battle Campaigns (Echoes of Silence, DVD), and accounts by those who were there.

April 2

On April 2nd, the day after Easter, General Mark Clark visited with the 442nd and addressed the members of the 100th Battalion. All was in readiness now for the offensive to begin. Later, veterans would think back on this time with pride in having been a small part of something that was larger than any one of them individually. World War II was, as Gen Dwight David Eisenhower, the Supreme Commander of Allied Forces in Europe called it, the "Great Crusade" and young men like Stanley Hayami were doing their part to win the peace. Perhaps it was this sense of the greater good that gave them the courage for the day-to-day horrors they would face. Stan was one of the thousands of untested, as well as seasoned, troops who were readied for battle.

April 3

On April 3 the 442nd RCT went from "rest" to "combat." They were the western arm of General Clark's pincer plan. The 100th Battalion was to attack frontally while the 3rd Battalion would attack from the East. They were to create a pincer inside the pincer. That night the men of the 100th Battalion moved west toward the village of Vallecchia where they would remain concealed until the next night.

At the same time those in the 3rd Battalion were loaded into trucks that moved under cover of darkness. At 9 o'clock, 2100 hours in army terms, their headlights were switched from dim to complete blackout. There was silence as the men climbed into the trucks and crouched with their heavy gear. They sweated from the heat of their gear and steel helmets. A cloud of dust rose from the roadway as the trucks slowly and silently as possible made their way in the foothills toward the outskirts of Pietrasanta. The black night sky lit up with white flashes exploding from artillery guns, their booming sounds grew ever louder and closer.

That night the 3rd Battalion and the 100th took the lead while Stan and soldiers of the 2nd Battalion were held in reserve. Typically, two of the three battalions, the 100th, the 3rd, or the 2nd, went into action while one remained in reserve. This kind of leapfrog strategy gave the men time to rest and rearm. Although Stanley and the 2nd Battalion were not at the front in the first day of the offensive, in the days and weeks ahead they often took a lead position as either the 100th or the 3rd Battalion moved into reserve.

Outside of Pietrasanta, the Nisei soldiers silently jumped out of the trucks and waited for the order to move out. Soon the only sound was that of their shuffling feet as they marched in single file on either side of the road.

Word was passed quietly to stay on the road, the shoulders were mined. As they moved forward the road became little more than a rocky trail that zigged and zagged uphill for eight long miles. Ahead were jagged mountains that soared two to three thousand feet, mountains they would have to scale in the darkness of night. On their backs the men carried sleeping rolls and two days ration plus their regular combat gear that weighed 100–120 pounds or more.

It was an arduous climb—seven hours of struggling as they pushed to reach the little village of Azzano, where they would stay concealed for the day. The dark, overcast night was made even more miserable with a steady drizzling rain. Along the trail there were steep drops 15–150 feet and streams that made the rocks underfoot slippery. Basic training had taught them to work as a unit, so that night they formed a "human chain" holding on to one another. Even that did not save many from falling. Twenty-five men were injured in falls down rocky cliffs. Those who fell did so in silence, so as not to give their position away.

April 4

Exhausted from their climb, they slept in houses in the village of Azzano. Through the daylight hours of April 4th they kept out of sight. More troops followed on the 4th with rations and supplies that had to be brought with a 30 mule train and 30 Italian civilian carriers. On the night of the 4th the men of the 3rd Battalion moved out of Azzano, down a narrow path, through an icy cold creek, over slippery boulders until at last they reached the bottom of Mt Carchio. Now they began another climb on a barren slope that gave little cover. They managed the treacherous perpendicular climb by holding on to roots of shrubs that dotted the mountainside. More than one man fell as they struggled to reach the ridgeline between Mt. Carchio and Mt. Folgorito. In full battle gear they crawled over the rocks on hands and knees. They darkened their faces and hands with soot and taped their metal dogtags, ID tags, on their necks, so that they would not make a sound. For eight hours they struggled to climb another shale mountainside that soared 3,000 feet high, struggling to keep their footing as they moved up 60 degree inclines in the darkness.

That same night the 100th moved silently into position for their frontal attack from the south. That night the 2nd Battalion followed the route to Pietrasanta, as the others had done, and from there they began a climb to Vallecchia.

April 5

Before daybreak on the 5th of April, the Nisei soldiers waited for the signal to begin firing. The enemy soldiers in their concrete bunkers were unaware that they were about to be attacked. It was no secret that German machineguns and mortars waited for those who approached and little doubt that many Nisei would surely be killed and maimed. But that night the Germans were sleeping.

This was one time in his life when Stanley had little time to write. We don't have Stanley's voice to tell us what he was feeling and thinking, but we can assume that his feelings were not vastly different from so many who recalled those days in oral histories; memories recorded long after the events for the Go For Broke Website at www.goforbroke.org.

For both the replacements and those with experience, the waiting was hard. "Old-timers," like Hachiro John Togashi, knew that their nervous fear could be the worst part. Once the battle began there was no time for anticipation. "You know someone is going to get hurt in combat . . . You hope the bullet or mortar shell doesn't have your name on it. You can't survive unless you're a fatalist!"

Hachiro John Togashi, Oral History, GoForBroke.org

Hiomi Suehiro, a young volunteer of the 100th Battalion, recalled his own fears while waiting for the battle to begin. Hiomi firmly believed it was "Better to die than be a coward. And disgrace my family or be the first man in the 100th to be a coward. So I kept repeating that over and over again. Better to die. And then I remembered a letter from my mother so I took the letter out . . .the letter started out with the usual salutations, everybody's fine, how are you . . . And as I

164

read her letter, . . . she said to me what can only be said from a mother to her son. She said, " . . .soon you will be fighting the enemy. My son, do not be a coward. Be brave for your father and your family." She knew from the day I volunteered that someday she would have to say the words that she said to me in her letter, "Don't disgrace my husband and your family," and I said to myself, how I can hurt her by being a coward? So I made a silent vow to her."

Hiomi Suehiro, Oral History, GoForBroke.org

By now, their letters home had been written, they had smoked their last cigarette, and prayed whatever prayer gave them strength to face what would follow. Some tucked a final letter home into a pocket, to be found in the event that they did not get there themselves. They checked their pockets for lucky charms, took a last look at photos of a girlfriend, a wife, a child. They checked their weapons one last time, waiting for the order to move out.

On April 5th at 6 o'clock in the morning, before the Italian sun rose, the Germans awoke to a 10 minute long barrage of artillery that thundered through the valley. The men of the German Kesselring Machinegun Battalion, known as some of Germany's finest gunners, were under siege and surprised to discover that the 442nd had returned to Italy. The battle had begun. Enemy mortars and machinegun fire rained down on the Nisei.

This was the start of a battle that would go on for almost a month of fighting with terrible losses, day after day. Nothing in their training could prepare them for the seemingly endless misery they faced as they wiped out one nest of German gunners with grenades, only to face yet another bunker further along the rocky grey hillsides. Often they had no cover except to hunker down in the holes created by shells lobbed at them from above.

From the hills they named Georgia, Florida, and Ohio 1, 2, 3; to the soaring marble mountains of Cerreta, Folgorita, Carchio, Belvedere, and Altissimo the 442nd had to fight their way from ridge to ridge. One mountain led to another still taller mountain that the Nisei needed to take control of as they advanced northward.

More than 60 years later, Norman Ikari still remembers the terror of shelling from the German 88s. The 88s were anti-aircraft/anti-tank guns that could penetrate an armored tank 2 km away and shoot high explosive shells.

Ikari has never forgotten " . . .the first time I ever heard one of those things come in . . .you hear this sort of instantaneous scream of a shell, high whistling scream. And then in a fraction of a second it explodes. And all you hope is that it doesn't explode near you . . . to be caught in an 88 barrage is a fearful frightening thing. Saw some pretty close hits, my company. And of course the farther down you're dug in the better you are. Of course this won't protect you if you get a direct hit because guys have been killed without any shrapnel wounds or anything like that. Just got killed from the close concussion of the explosion of the 88 shell near their foxhole. So, this is, this is the way it went for frontline men, day to day."

Norman Ikari ,Oral History, GoForBroke.org.

"War," as one man put it, "is 24 hours, everyday. You know, you see guys get blown up, you don't know when you gonna get killed either."

Choichi Shimabukuro, Oral History, GoForBroke.org

The terrain was not only high but also terrifying because you never knew when a sniper or machinegun would suddenly open fire or if you might slip and fall. For new replacements like Stan, the experience had to be even more horrifying because as they advanced, they saw all the wounded and dead of both sides, most were young men like themselves barely past 18 years old. For the first time, some were confronted with the reality, that they, like their friends in the 100th and the 3rd Battalion, might soon be one of the dead or dying being carried down the mountains.

Inevitably there were casualties. Decades later more than one Nisei veteran is still haunted with the grief of such sights. "The bad part is," Ray Nosaka recalls, "we just see them . . .you just keep going. We cannot stop for them. That's the hardest part, you know. Even that's your closest, closest buddy, you cannot stop for them. You got to advance, keep going. And then the medics will come . . . for every forty people, there's only one medic. So you can imagine—how can he take care, you know, when you get a barrage, about fifteen of them lying down. How can anybody . . . take care of all of them? So, the one that is seriously wounded, they try to take care of first. But you don't know how serious each one is. So somebody is going to bleed to death. Too late, you know. But sometimes, combat too, you know, you feel, you feel unlucky, you going to die. If you feel lucky, you, you survive."

Ray Nosaka, Oral History, GoForBroke.org

On that first day, 30 Germans were killed, many more were wounded or captured. They also lost 12 bunkers, 17 machineguns, and 3 big cannons. In 32 minutes, the 442nd had made the first breech in the Gothic Line! It would take many more days of battle to break all of the enemy's defenses. Yet, the Nisei had done what they always did. They had done what others failed to do. The Germans knew them as a formidable force. The Gothic Line was not won, but it had been broken!

The Nisei victory was not won cheaply. Many Nisei died and were wounded that day. 19 men were killed in action (KIA). Company K had 100 casualties alone. It took seven hours and sixteen different relay teams to take the wounded out of these forward positions down terrifyingly steep mountainsides.

One soldier, Sadao Munemori, made history in that battle, as the first Japanese American to receive the country's highest award for military valor, the Medal of Honor. He was a Nisei from Los Angeles imprisoned with his family in Manzanar internment camp. When his squad leader was wounded, Pfc. Munemori led several solo attacks, wiping out two machine guns with grenades. While he sought safety in a shell crater with two comrades, an unexploded grenade bounced off his helmet, rolling toward them. By smothering the grenade's blast with his body, he saved the lives of his comrades. He received the Medal of Honor posthumously. Although many other soldiers of the 442nd deserved that award, Munemori's was the only one awarded to the Nisei troops during WWII. It took another 55 years before other Nisei would receive Medals of Honor for their heroic deeds during World War II.

The 442nd was not the only segregated unit in the war, in fact at the start of this campaign the Nisei troops were attached to the 92nd Infantry Division, the only African American infantry division to see combat in Europe during W.W.II. Known as the "Buffalo Soldiers," they too were segregated by race and were also discriminated against when it came to the highest awards.

April 6–8

On April 6th the 442nd continued their assault of the enemy. With surprising speed they secured the ridges from Georgia to Mt. Folgorita. They now controlled Mt. Cerreta and Mt. Carchio. By the end of the day, just two mountains, Mt. Belvedere and Mt. Altissimo were all that remained of the German's hold of the Gothic Line. That night, Stan and the 2nd Battalion did their own all night climb and without time to sleep, they made a full-scale assault on the well-fortified Mt. Belvedere at dawn on April 7th. For hours they were pinned down by mortar fire while the crack Kesserling Machine Gun Battalion fought to defend its stronghold.

Yukio Okutsu, a courageous Technical Sergeant who finally took it upon himself to single handedly destroy three machine gun nests, allowing his men to once again take the offensive. By nightfall the 442nd was in command of all the ridges! Now they continued to move Northeast, climbing mountains, destroying enemy fortifications, taking prisoners and small towns along the way.

Nisei soldiers were shocked to find that the enemy troops they killed or took as prisoners included boys as young as 14 to 15, as well as men older than their fathers. By April 8th the Allies controlled the highway on the Western coast and continued to push the enemy off the Gothic Line. They began taking one town after another where civilians greeted them warmly. But the war was not over.

Fog and rain added to their difficulties and enemy coastal guns fired at those carrying ammo, water, and rations to the front. Supplies had to be moved under cover of darkness. On April 8th, the losses were bitter as 8 Nisei were killed. Enemy sharpshooters easily picked off the determined young men of the 442nd, as they mounted a slow, costly advance along the twisting rocky paths that offered little shelter. Bursts of enemy fire not only sent bullets flying, the bullets bounced onto rocks that splintered and turned into shrapnel that cut into the limbs and lives of too many young soldiers. Still the Nisei men moved forward through minefields and brutal rounds of machine gun fire. More than half of their injuries were caused by hard-to-see mines.

April 9–13

On April 9th, Stan's 2nd Battalion, Company E, waged a fierce battle to take Pariana, a small village where survivors of the Kesserling Machinegun Battalion were holding out. Fighting went on all day and into the night. On the 10th of April the Germans in the village surrendered. Only 62 of the 150 Germans had survived. The Nisei captured 8 machine guns, and 12 mortars.

By Friday the 13th it seemed that the Germans were on the run. Stan, with the 2nd Battalion, was chasing the enemy in retreat. What they did not know was that the Germans high up on another mountain saw them coming. Just as they reached the base of Mount Pizzacuto the Germans opened fire and pinned down the men of the 2nd Battalion. Before it was over, 5 Americans were killed in action and 5 more were wounded. They won the battle, but victory was still elusive. The Germans continued fighting while destroying fortifications, roads, and bridges as they retreated.

April 14–18

The 442nd had been on the move for more than two weeks when Stanley was able to write a V-mail to his family. His 2nd Battalion was again in reserve and hot meals were brought up to the weary troops—a luxury after days of K rations. Stan wrote a short message, but between the lines one can sense that he is close to the front. By now, Stanley and all the replacements had become "old-timers." They had survived, but the battle was still not won.

The V-mail that follows, dated April 18th, was not mailed until April 30th.

April 18, 1945
Italy

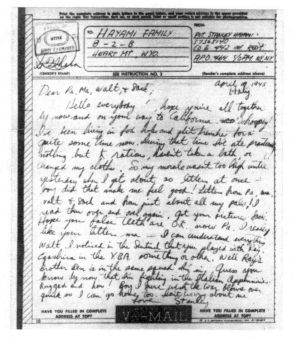

Dear Pa, Ma, Walt & Sach,

Hello everybody! Hope you're all together by now and on your way to California. Whoopey! I've been lying in fox holes and slit trenches for quite some time now. During that time I ate practically nothing but K rations, haven't taken a bath, or changed my clothes. So my morale wasn't too high until yesterday when I got about 20 letters at once—boy did that make me feel good! Letters from Pa, Ma, Walt & Sach and about all my pals! I read them over and over again. Got your picture, Sach. Hope your false teeth are O.K. now Pa. I really like your letter Ma—I can understand everything. Walt, I noticed in the Sentinel that you played with Roy

Ogashin in the Y.B.A. something or other. Well Rays brother Ben in the same squad I'm in. Guess you know by now that I'm fighting in the Italian Apennines.. Rugged and how! Boy I sure wish the war blows over quick so I can go home too. Don't worry about me.

Love
Stanley

April 19–20

But the war did not "blow over quick," as Stan put it. The next day, April 19th, the 442nd was ordered to press on and take the city of Aulla where the Germans were staging a near final defense. There was just one way for the Allied forces to defeat them in Aulla and that was to make their way over hills that were heavily defended with mortars and machine gun fire. The 442nd lost 5 men on the 19th, and four more on the 20th.

April 21

On the 21st word came that the Germans were withdrawing elsewhere, but in the area of Tendola, ahead of them, the enemy was dug in and had reinforcements. The 442nd would have to fight every step of the way to reach Aulla.

On the 21st, Stanley with the 2nd Battalion, Company E, was in the vicinity of San Terenzo, a town in the hills of Tuscany. They were on the crest of a well-fortified hill, Colle Musatello, when entrenched enemy forces in bunkers greeted them with a hail of machine gun fire.

As he remembers it, Daniel K. Inouye, then a 20-year old Second Lieutenant, who led Stan's platoon, readied his men for the attack, though he had a premonition that all was not well. As he always did, he put his hand into his shirt pocket—it was empty. Now he was even more uneasy. Until then he had always carried two "lucky" silver dollars in that pocket. Weeks earlier, after a battle in France, he'd discovered one coin was cracked and the other was bent by a German bullet. Exactly where the coins had been, there were bruises on his chest—proof that his "lucky charms" had saved his life. Now they were gone. Despite his sense of impending disaster, the young officer led his men into battle and directed his platoon through a storm of enemy fire.

Stan was among those who managed to capture a mortar position and moved very close to the enemy on Colle Musatello. Their 3rd platoon was well ahead of the others and Lt. Inouye had to make a decision; whether to wait for the 1st and 2nd platoons to reach them or to attack.

Lt. Inouye went ahead of his men. He took a grenade from his belt and was about to throw it. At that moment, a terrible pain hit his side. Ignoring the pain he counted down to three and threw the grenade. Seeing the enemy pulling out he signaled his men to come forward. His men realized he had been wounded, but the young officer continued to pursue the enemy, managing to throw two more grenades that silenced a second enemy machinegun. Although he was wounded, Lt. Inouye continued to fight. He and his men charged forward to take out a third machine gun.

Despite his wounds, Lt. Inouye pulled the pin on his last grenade and stood up to hurl it at the enemy. In that split second, the enemy spotted him and fired a rifle grenade at him. Inouye looked down to see his arm barely hanging on and in his hand, that he could no longer control, he was still clutching the grenade. His men tried to come forward to help him, but he told them to go back. He managed in that moment to use his good hand to pry free the grenade and threw it. Despite his terrible wound and the intense pain, he continued to direct his platoon until he was hit again, in the leg and the stomach, and he rolled down a hillside.

Hours later, doctors were unable to save Daniel Inouye's arm and with that loss he gave up his dream of becoming a doctor. For his incredible bravery, Daniel Inouye was awarded the Distinguished Service Cross, the second highest medal of the US Army. 55 years later, in 2000, the DSC was upgraded to a Medal of Honor after re-examination of the records.

Although the Germans knew they were defeated, those who fought on were desperately trying to buy time for small detachments of their men to escape. Fighting with them were Italian fascists who had refused to surrender even though Italy had surrendered. Other battles raged in the mountains on that misty April day and many saw friends fall wounded or killed. This was one of the great miseries of the battlefield. There were also the sorrowful sounds of the injured pleading for help from the medics or calling for their mothers in English, German, Japanese, and Italian.

By nightfall of the 21st another 12 Nisei had died and scores more were being taken down the mountains wounded. Slipping and sliding up and down rocky paths, the litter bearers did their best to move those for whom the war was over. But for the 442nd the fighting continued. From the start, they moved along the mountains behind but parallel to the coast.

April 22

For young men like Stanley this had to be a terrifying time, seeing friends maimed or worse and wondering if the next bullet, shell, or toe popper landmine would be for them. Many GIs in such situations became shell shocked and mentally unable to go on fighting. For the boys of the 442nd running away or quitting was not a choice. They had something to prove to themselves, their families, and their country. The Germans were retreating, but the deadly fight continued.

Attacks continued from the north and south against Tendola. Sixty German soldiers were taken prisoner that day, but six members of the 442nd were killed in action.

Technical Sergeant Gordon Takasaki replaced Daniel Inouye as the leader of Stan's unit, the 3rd Platoon. Takasaki had participated in every campaign of the Go For Broke unit: Rome-Arno, Battle of Bruyeres and Lost Battalion, Southern France-Champagne Campaign, and now in the Po Valley Campaign.

April 23

On April 23rd, Stan, along with the 2nd Battalion, Company E was ordered to take the village of San Terenzo, a well-fortified Tuscan village. He was with the 3rd Platoon that attacked Hill 303, flanking the town from the east, while the 2nd Platoon pushed into the town itself from the south. Company G took a hill further to the east.

San Terenzo was fiercely defended not only by Germans but by Italian sharpshooters, the *Bersaglieri,* who had refused to surrender when Italy and most of its army were defeated in 1943. They fought along with German soldiers who were also ordered to fight on, although the outcome was already certain. Hitler's ambitions for his "master race" were dead, as he would be in another week, but the final bloody battles of the war in Europe were not over yet.

It's unlikely that Stan or his buddies were thinking of Hitler or world events. There, in the bleak rainy days of April, high in the Apennine Mountains, these young soldiers were weary from weeks of non-stop combat. They were thousands of miles from home, families, and their civilian lives. From one moment to the next, they were dealing with the terror of killing or being killed. These teenaged boys, who should have been going to college, cheering at a football game, driving their jalopies, dancing the jitterbug, these young inexperienced GIs were expected to fight like men.

For weeks the 442nd Regimental Combat Team had taken terrible losses as they took hundreds of enemy prisoners and one little town and mountain after another. Still they forged on. "Go for Broke!" was not just a motto—it was the battle cry of the 442nd—the determined will they brought to every encounter, to give their all, proving for all time that they were loyal Americans.

Company E, 2nd Battalion made their way into the usually quiet little mountain town of San Terenzo. But on the 23rd of April there was no quiet in San Terenzo. According to Italian accounts a patrol of Nisei soldiers entered the church and pointed their guns at the parish priest and the parishioners until the priest convinced them that they were not sheltering any enemy soldiers in the church.

Technical Sergeant Gordon Kiyoshi Takasaki led Stan and the men of the 3rd platoon into San Terenzo, maneuvering to capture a dominating ridge. As the Germans desperately attempted to pull out, Takasaki led his men to cut off their escape route. Among the records of those who died in the Second World War, there is an eyewitness account of what happened next to Stan's new Sergeant:

> Through heavy German mortar machine gun and artillery fire, Technical Sergeant Takasaki advanced exposing himself to heavy fire in his attempt to surround and disorganize the enemy. Wounded in the chest by machine gun fire, he continued to direct his men in battle. Refusing aid for himself in favor of his wounded men, he summoned his remaining strength to continue the fight. As a result of his plans and orders, his men cut the enemy escape road and brilliantly accomplished their mission. Sergeant Takasaki died in the last major campaign of the 442nd.
>
> *Echoes of Silence CD, KIA Profiles, 2nd Battalion*

Kelly Kuwayama, who was a medic with the 3rd Platoon, E Company was beside Sgt. Takasaki when he was killed by sniper fire. He remembers that the same bullet hit the man behind the sergeant, who was directing his men through a mortar barrage and machine gun fire. Sgt. Takasaki "encouraged his men to go through that fire, exposing himself." Kuwayama also recalled that in combat the sergeants may have been told where they are going, what they are doing, but to the men: "One hill became indistinguishable from the next. All I knew was that we were to take the hill and a machine gun was shooting at us. I did not know Hill 303 as such."

Kelly Kuwayama e-mail to author, August 2007

Roy Kawamoto, who shipped out to Europe with Stan and served in Company E, was injured on that same day. Years later Roy told his son, Ken, that in the midst of battle, a big Hawaiian soldier picked him up and carried him to safety on his back. Bullets were flying and for a moment his rescuer did not move. Roy recalled how he put his hands over the Hawaiian soldier's eyes and just shouted, "Keep running!"

Ken Kawamoto interview with author, May 2007

The bloody battle in and around San Terenzo had been going on for days. After hours of brutal fighting on the 23rd there was a brief truce when the crackle of the machine guns ceased. White flags were raised, allowing time to aid those who were wounded. Some recall a hush that spread through the valley that was soon filled with the sad voices of the wounded. They spoke in many languages but the sound of pain was the same.

Before long the fighting resumed, continuing well into the evening when the enemy forces were surrounded. The 442nd took San Terenzo as well as 115 prisoners, six artillery radios, 30 bicycles, 25 horses and mules. 40 enemy soldiers were dead.

It had been another day of terrible losses for the 442nd. On the 23rd of April six more Nisei were Killed in Action.

The first name on the list is Stanley K. Hayami.

Those who fought at Stanley's side reported what happened this way . . .

There were two platoons advancing to attack the village of San Terenzo, under hostile machine gun and sniper fire.

After a short firefight, one platoon drove the enemy from its objective, a ridge to the right of the village. The other platoon advanced, in an encircling movement, but was pinned down on open terrain by crossfire from four hostile machine guns.

In the ensuing fire-fight, many men of the platoon were wounded by enemy fire. Pvt. Hayami left his covered position and crept toward the wounded men. Despite the hostile machine gun and sniper fire directed at him, he reached the first casualty.

Exposing himself in a kneeling position, he administered first aid and then proceeded to another man and rendered first aid without regard for the foe's heavy fire. While engaged in this act he was mortally wounded. Pvt. Hayami's unselfish courage under such hazardous combat conditions reflects credit upon the finest traditions of the United States Army.

(Citation for the Bronze Star and Purple Heart awarded posthumously to Stanley.)

****

There is no way of knowing the names of the two soldiers Stanley tried to rescue or if either of them survived. All searches for records and eyewitnesses have led to the same answer: not available. Unfortunately, all such official records were lost in a fire at the National Archives in St. Louis in 1973. All that we do know is that Stanley made a choice to defend his country. In doing so, he dedicated himself to protecting those with whom he pledged to serve. His heroic action was typical of the brave young men of the 100th/442nd Regimental Combat Team that won more awards for their sacrifices than any other unit of their size in United States Army history.

The V-mail, written on the 18th of April, filled with its longing for home, was the final letter Stanley Hayami wrote. It was postmarked April 30, 1945. His family did not yet know what had happened to Stanley.

Stanley died on April 23rd, just two days before the United Nations Conference began, a meeting to write the UN charter. That first meeting was in San Francisco, in the state Stanley had longed to return to. Yet, even today, his dream of a United Nations of Earth is yet to be realized.

****

News of Stanley's death did not reach the Hayami family for weeks!

In fact the war in Europe was over and the Hayami family celebrated V-E (Victory in Europe) Day on May 8th, not knowing what had happened to their son.

Stan's good friend Tadao Takano was visiting his own family in Heart Mountain. Tad had always spent a lot of time with the Hayamis before he and Stan left, so he naturally went to see Stan's family. In fact, Tad was at Heart Mountain on May 8th, when V-E Day arrived. The war in Europe was over! Tad recalls Stan's mother on that day . . .

> When the war was won I remember his mother telling me that she was greatly relieved because Stanley was safe (his older brother had been wounded earlier). I had returned to Heart Mountain from Washington University in St. Louis. By then I had been drafted and I was awaiting induction in June 1945.
>
> One afternoon, I was playing basketball by myself when a next-door neighbor told me that there was 'something wrong' at the Hayamis.

> *Tadao Takano interview with author, April 2005*

On May 9th, one day after all the celebrations, the joy of V-E Day was turned to shock and grief. A Western Union Telegram arrived at Heart Mountain and was delivered to Block 8-Building 2-Unit B . . .

Stanley died in action a few weeks before the war in Europe was over, but

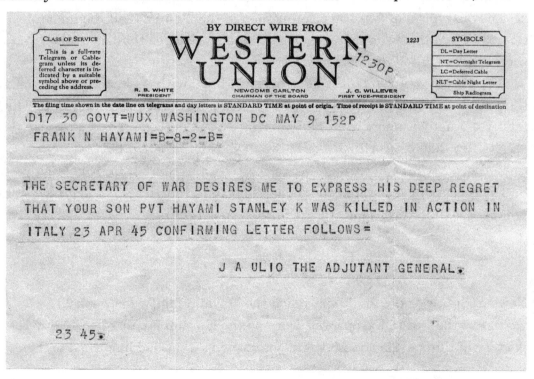

his family was not notified until 2 weeks after his death. He died on one of the last days of organized resistance in Italy! The war in Italy ended officially on May 2nd. The war in Europe ended on May 8th, the day before the telegram arrived. Too late for Stan and the Hayami family.

Tad confesses that he can never forget the terrible sorrow he felt. He recalls going to dinner with the Hayamis at the block mess hall where he broke down uncontrollably. In fact, he remembers that they tried to put on a brave face, but they all wept.

Although more than 60 years have passed, Walt could still recall the day the news came. "I remember coming home and my mother sitting there and crying . . .in fact, my mother and dad were both there . . .and my dad told me that Stanley was killed . . . they had gotten a telegram."

Walt said his parents were not bitter, but deeply grieved. They had to be in shock as well. Sach had already gone ahead of the family to California, excited about getting set up and returning to their home. They naturally assumed that both Frank and Stanley had survived the war and would be joining them before long. It is hard to imagine the shock of that telegram coming two weeks later.

Soon after that terrible time, when they talked of Stanley's death, Sach and her mother discovered that they both had the same dream on the same night in April. Both of them dreamed that Stanley had come to them asking for a glass of water . . . it was the night that Stanley died.

Frank received the news long before the official telegram was sent to Heart Mountain. In fact, Frank was in the same battle. When it was over, he suffered the terrible sorrow of seeing Stan's body before he was taken away for burial.

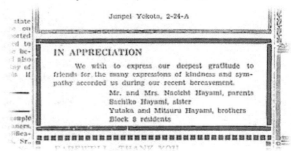

Hayami family's note of appreciation published in the Heart Mountain Sentinel.

Frank's letter begins with the bittersweet news that the war in Italy ended just days earlier. Written in script, it looks different from the bold printed letters he sent earlier. It does not begin with the usual breezy salutation of "Dear folks . . . "

His short tender letter, addressed and written to his mother, speaks for itself . . .

May 7
Italy

Dear Mother:

I am fine and well. We are now resting. The war is over for us for the present. Now we have to salute all officers, keep clean at all times, have our clothes always buttoned, etc. Just like the days back in Shelby.

Thank you for the money. It's going to come in handy. I sent you and Grace four pairs of silk stocking.

My heart goes to you in our great loss. Have faith and courage — for god now has him in tender care. Rest assured that I'm trying to do all that I can over here.

I'll write again later.

your loving son
Frank

Years later, Frank wrote again about these events . . .

My younger brother, Stan, was drafted right out of the Heart Mountain Concentration Camp at the age of 18, and he and I were wounded in the same action in Italy. He died of wounds suffered in battle, dead at the age of 19. I was luckier. My mother received that fateful telegram from the Army informing her of the death of her 19-year old son while still in Heart Mountain Concentration Camp. My mother became a Gold Star mother, not in the comfortable surroundings of her California home, but in the stark harsh concentration camp room set in the Wyoming desert, while still denied the right to American citizenship and access to her home.

There was a Christian church using one of the empty barracks for church service every Sunday. The Reverend Donald Toriumi officiated at the English services and Reverend Unoura presided over the Japanese speaking service . . . And it was here in the barren barrack church that funeral services were held for my brother Stanley, when my mother was advised that he had been killed in action on April 23, 1945 in Italy fighting with the 442nd Regimental Combat team. His body was buried in a cemetery outside of Bologna, Italy. In late 1949, his body, as well as those of three others, were brought back to the Los Angeles area at which time a full blown funeral service complete with military personnel with Colonel John Aiso in charge was held at the Los Angeles Union Church.

Frank Hayami letter to Mike Mackey, Oct. 16, 1992

The news of Stanley's death spread as it was on the front page of the Heart Mountain Sentinel of Saturday May 12, 1945. Not only was Stanley dead, the paper says that Frank Hayami was injured in the same battle. We have no details about Frank's injuries. His army records, like Stan's and those of many

HEART MOUNTAIN

Vol. IV No. 20   Heart Mountain, Wyoming Saturday, May 12, 1945

Stan Hayami, '44 Grad, Falls in Italian Action; Pvt. Kawamoto Wounded

Pvt. Stanley K. Hayami, son of Mr. and Mrs. Frank N. Hayami, 8-2-B, last year graduate of Heart Mountain high school, was killed in action in Italy April 23, according to information received this week from the War department.

One other Heart Mountain youth, Pvt. Roy Kawamoto, son of James Kawamoto, 9-19-E, was reported slightly wounded in Italy the same day, it was announced here.

Both soldiers were inducted into the armed services in June, 1944.

The death of Private Hayami came as a double blow to the Hayami family since another son, Pfc. Frank Y. Hayami, was reported wounded in Italy on April 23.

At Heart Mountain high school Private Hayami was an outstanding student and served as art editor of Tempo, the 1944 yearbook. He was a talented artist and was largely responsible for the illustrations of the annual publication.

Before coming to Heart Mountain, Private Hayami attended Mark Keppel high school at San Gabriel, Calif., where his father was a prominent nurseryman at 617 East Valley boulevard.

Besides his mother and father and brother Frank, the soldier is survived by another brother, Walter, now attending school here, and a sister, Grace, formerly secretary in the community management division, now in Pasadena.

Private Kawamoto formerly lived on route three, 275 Los Gatos, Calif.

He attended Campbell high school and later San Jose state college.

Devers Gives Cpl. Tsutsumi Bronze Medal

HEADQUARTERS 6TH ARMY GROUP—Gen. Jacob L. Devers, commanding general of the 6th army group this week announced the awarding of a Bronze Star medal to Cpl. Noburu Tsutsumi of Heart Mountain, Wyo. Besides Corporal Tsutsumi five other nisei soldiers from relocation centers were similarly honored.

Corporal Tsutsumi, formerly of White Salmon, Wash., entered the army in May, 1943 as a volunteer. His sister, Mrs. Tom Sagara, 21-4-EF, and an aunt, Mrs. S. Nakagawa, 23-6-B, lives at Heart Mountain, Wyo.

Following is Corporal Tsutsumi's citation: ". . . for heroic achievement in the vicinity of Il Terricio, Italy, on 6 July, 1944. When an enemy barrage severed the communication line leading to a forward element, Corporal Tsutsumi voluntarily repaired and restored its function. Subsequently, when communications again became disrupted, he proceeded into the impact area, made the necessary repairs, and remained in his hazardous position for the next hour in order to keep the communication line intact."

Following are the other citations: Tech. Sgt. Albert K. Na-

One-Thi Have Fi To Leav

GI Fathers' Greetings Must Be Mailed May 15

With outgoing soldier mail volume now in excess of 40,-000,000 individual pieces a week, the War Department today urged the wives and children of American soldiers serving overseas who are contemplating the sending of Father's Day greetings to get them into the mails between now and May 15 in order to assure delivery prior to Father's Day, June 17, 1945.

Bank Accounts Unblocked by US Treasury

WASHINGTON, D.C.—To aid WRA in its relocation and liquidation program, the Treasury department has informed the WRA that they will unblock all but a limited number of the accounts of evacuees on the army clear list.

Through the project director, forms to request unblocking orders will be forwarded to the Federal Reserve bank in San Francisco. The bank will determine whether the statements on the individual forms are correct. Individual unblocking orders will be mailed in care of the project director, and private banks will be notified.

other men of the 442nd, were lost in the great fire in the National Archives.

The same newspaper article reports that Roy Kawamoto had been slightly injured in the same battle in Italy. It's possible that Roy was one of the buddies Stan went to rescue when the Italian sharpshooters cut him down.

Memorial Service at Heart Mountain.

"In peace, sons bury their fathers. In war, fathers bury their sons."
—Herodotus

The next week, Guy Robertson, WRA Director of Heart Mountain, paid tribute to Stanley and 5 other young men who had given their lives in battle. The Boy Scout Drum and Bugle Corps opened the ceremony with an overture. Wreaths were laid before the Gold Star flag by Camp Fire and Girl Scouts while the Boy Scouts band played "Nearer My God to Thee."

****

Walt recalled his family's return to San Gabriel . . .

> There was still a great deal of negative feeling toward the Nikkei before they returned. There was a family that went back before we did and one of the daughters in that family said it was quite hostile for Japanese Americans until the word came about Stanley. And they made an announcement in the assembly. After that, she said things changed quite a bit. So in that sense, some good came out of it.
>
> *Walter Hayami interview with author, Nov. 4, 2004*

It was a terrible price to pay for acceptance. Walt attended Mark Keppel High

School where many teachers remembered Stanley with great fondness. In fact, Walt brought the diary to Stanley's English teacher, Miss Maud Hudson. She read it and wanted it to be published, so that in some small way Stanley's dreams and promise would live on, despite the general public's lack of knowledge or concern about the camps and the people incarcerated in them. That was shortly after the war and there was no interest in publishing anything about the incarceration at that time.

Many Americans didn't want to acknowledge what had happened to the Japanese Americans during the war and how unjust and illegal it was. For some it was simply racism or a belief that every Japanese American, even babies and the elderly, must have done something to "deserve" such treatment. For others it was blind faith that the US Government would never have done something like that to its own citizens. Even today there are some people that deny that the internment ever happened. Perhaps this deliberate ignorance is just an excuse that some people use to avoid confronting the truth.

In 1952, President Harry Truman signed the McCarran-Walter Act, finally abolishing the laws that had prevented Asian immigrants from becoming naturalized citizens of the United States. Thousands of Issei fulfilled a dream that had been on hold for decades. Naoichi and Asano Hayami were among the first to raise their hands, taking the oath to become American citizens. The Hayami family rebuilt their nursery, but it was a struggle as big agri-businesses were changing the nature of farming in the postwar world. For the Hayamis, and so many of the Issei generation, life would never be the same.

Many years later, when Asano Hayami was quite old, one of her granddaughters, Judy Hayami, had the diary translated into Japanese. Decades had passed; now for the first time his mother could read Stanley's words. After so many years, it was a bittersweet treasure for his mother. She had saved all of his letters, but his diary gave her both joy and sorrow. Stanley's dreams and hopes for a future that had been lost and would never be fulfilled, moved her to tears.

According to Walt, even before the war, Stan was always starting diaries. He'd start with a New Year's resolution, but he never finished them. This one he finished, giving us a glimpse into the incarceration; a time and place that must never be forgotten, so that it will never happen again.

Stan really wanted to go to college, to have the opportunity to explore the world of ideas and his own potential. Like so many of his generation, time was not on his side. Instead of college dances and football games, he had to grow up fast and deal with things like death and killing. Instead of the lecture hall and library, he had to worry over toe popper landmines and sharpshooters hidden in the hillsides.

It is impossible to know what Stanley Hayami might have achieved had he returned from the battlefields of Europe. Young men like Stanley had their whole lives ahead of them. His possibilities were endless. He might have become a great artist, a peacemaker, a government leader, a writer, or a teacher. One of the great sorrows of war is that young people, who do most of the fighting, are also the ones who make the greatest sacrifices, giving up their dreams and lives along the way.

From the time he started his diary at the age of 16, until he gave his life at 19, serving his country, Stanley Hayami never surrendered his hopes for a better future. He did not get to fulfill his dreams. He knew all too well that we do not live in a perfect democracy with liberty and justice for all—not then, not now. But perhaps we can borrow from Stanley's aspirations, working to make his dream for a United Nations of Earth, a reality . . . a world where racism becomes a strange ugly thing of the past; a world where we find a common language to make peace, not war.

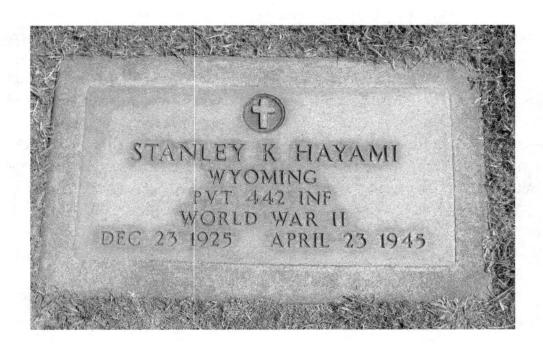

ACKNOWLEDGMENTS

My thanks to the California Civil Liberties Public Education Program for their support of this project along with the Japanese American National Museum that holds the rights to Stanley Hayami's diary. I'm grateful to those at the Japanese American National Museum who encouraged me in this work: Irene Hirano, President of JANM, to Sojin Kim, who answered endless questions, sent scans and suggestions, and commiserated over the many bumps along the way. Thanks to Cris Paschild who was on board with this project from the start, along with Karen Higa and John Guzman, who read the first draft, Allyson Nakamoto of the Education Department, for her helpful suggestions, Jane Nakasako of Hirasaki Resource Center, who found the immigration details about the Hayami family, and Snowden Becker who urged me to look at the diary in the first place.

I am indebted to the Hayami family. The late Walter Hayami, Stanley's younger brother, and his wife Miko, shared family stories with me at the start of this project, though it was not easy for them to speak of their losses. Miko also lost a brother, S/Sgt. James S. Karatsu, who was KIA in France in January 1945. Shortly before Walter's death, they found photographs, missing letters, and even did some translations. Special thanks to their son, Dan Hayami, who acted as central headquarters, passing e-mails back and forth and scanning photos.

Thanks to Tadao Takano, Stan's friend, who had such meaningful memories to share. I also spoke with Frank Hayami's wife, Martha, about her late husband, who worked as an Electrical Engineer in New York for all of his professional life after he left the Army. Sadly, Frank passed away shortly after I started this work, so we never met. I was also too late to meet their sister, Sach, who worked as a designer before she returned to California where she raised her family. I'm grateful to her daughter, Lisa Halverson, Stan's niece, for sharing some of her mother's story and her own thoughts about the uncle she never met. She knows him as a gentle soul from family stories that kept him alive in their hearts.

For preserving the history of the 100th/442nd RCT and helping me connect with veterans, I am indebted to Ellen Endo, Chief Operating Officer and Executive Director and President Christine Sato-Yamazaki of the Go For Broke National Education Center. Through the invaluable resources of the Center and their kind permission I was allowed to quote from the oral histories of men who were brothers in arms of Stanley. Mahalo to Joy Teraoka, Col. Bert Nishimura,

Andy Ono, Jimmy Yamashita, Walter Okitsu, Yeiichi (Kelly) Kuwayama, Lawson Sakai, Davide Del Giudice, Ron Yamada, and Roger Eaton who sent me records of the 100th/442nd and a narrative of the Po Valley Campaign by Shuji Taketomo. These documents and personal testimonies helped to tell the story of Stanley's last days.

I am indebted to Mike Mackey who generously shared letters he had collected for his books about life in Heart Mountain. Among them, I found the powerful letter by Frank Hayami that is included in this work. Sincere thanks, to Bacon Sakatani, who shared his knowledge and resources about Heart Mountain and to LaDonna Zall and the Heart Mountain Wyoming Foundation, for preserving the history of that time and place where so many courageous people struggled to make a life. Thanks to Aloha South and Charles Spencer at the National Archives for their 11th hour help in finding Stanley's cover photo and WRA records. Thanks to John Colby, James Oppenheim, and Joan Auclair, who contributed their enthusiasm and skills in creating Stanley's book.

My thanks to Philip Chin, who edited much of this manuscript and contributed much as it took shape. Thanks to those who generously read and commented on various drafts of the book: Sojin Kim, Allyson Nakamoto, Dr. Setsuko Matsunaga Nishi, Walter Okitsu, Dr. Carrie Sorensen, Dr. Patrick Westcott, Elaine Yamaguchi, Amy Sullivan, and Byron Thomas. Their insights added much to the final manuscript. Thanks to Dr. Masami Tamagawa, assistant professor of Japanese at Skidmore College, who met the challenge of making Stanley's letters readable without changing his non academic spelling. Any mistakes are my own.

My thanks to the Honorable Sen. Daniel Inouye, a hero of long standing, who has steadfastly reminded us that a love of our great country is not limited to any ethnic group and that this chapter in history should never be forgotten.

Finally I want to thank my dear husband, Stephen, who has read countless drafts, listened to endless stories, and still cheers me on.

Joanne Oppenheim,
New York City

NOTES

JANM ....Japanese American National Museum
NARA ....National Archives
HMS ....*Heart Mountain Sentinel*
SHD ....Stanley Hayami Diary
BSC ....Bacon Sakatani Collection
WRA...........................War Relocation Authority
442nd RCT ....442nd Regimental Combat Team

Introduction (PG. 5–14)

PG. 7 "For the next..." Issei men often sent to Japan for a "picture bride" as there were few Japanese women in America and they could not legally marry a Caucasian. Marriages were arranged in many cultures at the time and couples did not known each other until after they married.

 pg. 7 "For the next...." Stan's mother arrived on the *Anyo Maru*. It took 2 weeks to travel from Japan to the U.S.A. *Anyo* means Peace and *Maru* means ship. Years later, the ship was torpedoed and sunk on January 8, 1945 by the submarine, *USS Barb*.

PG. 8 "They were Issei..." The Chinese Exclusion Act dated back to 1882 and applied to all Asians.

PG. 9 "In signing that..." Memorandum from General DeWitt to the Secretary of War, U.S. War Department, Office of Chief of Staff, Final Report: Japanese Evacuation from the West Coast 1942" (Washington, D.C.: Government Printing Office, 1943).

PG. 13 "My full name..." Forty Heart Mountaineers shared their experiences with Mike Mackey, and his thesis became a book, *Heart Mountain, Life in Wyoming's Concentration Camp* (Western History Pub. 2000)

1942 (PG. 13–34)

PG. 18 "It had to..." Gene Krupa was a musician remembered for his wild drumming style that was copied by many drummers in both jazz and rock.

PG. 19 "I realize the..." Frank uses the term

Concentration Camp to describe relocation centers. The use of that term is controversial even today, associated as it is with the deaths of six million Jews and millions of other victims in Nazi death camps. In 1944, President Franklin Roosevelt, referred to relocation centers as concentration camps, meaning a "concentration" of the Japanese Americans as an ethnic group in camps. By Order of the President, Greg Robinson, Harvard University (Cambridge, MA, 2002)

PG. 21 "In fact, one..." Interviews with Teachers, Community Analysis, Sept 1, 1943.; War Relocation Authority (hereafter WRA), Reel 16, Record Group 210, U.S. National Archives, Washington, D.C. (hereafter NARA).

PG. 22 "I didn't write..." Sonja Henie was a multiple gold medal world and Olympic ice skating star who popularized the use of dance choreography and appeared in many movies that popularized winter sports.

PG. 23 "The temperature was..." Heart Mountain Shivers, *Heart Mountain Sentinel*, WY Newspapers, reel 62-33-241 (hereafter HMS) Jan. 23, 1943, 1.

PG. 25 "I remember my..." In Poston, a WRA Camps in Arizona, they would have suffered heat that hit 127 degrees that summer. In Heart Mt. winter came early with temperatures below zero.

PG. 26 "Tomorrow at Los..." Bill Stern was the best-known sportscaster of his time. In pre-TV days he was the eyes of radio listeners.

PG. 30 "Merry Xmas! Well..." The teams, Pomona and Santa Anita were named for two assembly centers.

PG. 32 "Gifts from outside..." In 1942, an average worker earned $1880 a year. But things were much cheaper then. The average cost of a house was $3770; a gallon of gas was 15 cents! A bottle of Coca Cola was a nickel, a car cost $920. But, even by 1942's standards, the salaries inside the camps were very low. thepeoplehistory.com

PG. 32 "I was just…"Pearl Buck suggests that loyal Japanese Americans might become future "governors, administrators, and democratic leaders in post war Japan." After Victory—What?, by Louis Adamic, *Scholastic Magazine*, Vol. 41, No. 12, December 7-12, 1942, 14-15.

PG. 33 "To Stan, the…" Those in the Military Intelligence Service (MIS) became translators, intercepting messages, and interrogating Japanese prisoners. Most MIS served in the Pacific, often close to the front where they might easily be mistaken as enemy. Their role was little known until long after the war. Maj. Gen. C.A. Willoughby, Ass't Chief of Staff, of the Far East Command, said MIS Nisei "saved over a million American lives and shortened the war by 2 years."

1943 (PG. 35–95)

PG. 37 "Prediction. War will…" Stan's prediction was right! The war went on for another year and a half!

PG. 41 "Inside the schools…" HMS, Jan 15, 1944. Some essays were about having more privacy, returning to more normal living, being with Caucasian friends. Many indicated that their parents do not want to go.

PG. 42 "Inside the camp…" Quote from Nob Shimokochi's interview with author, Nov. 2005. Photo shows students saluting with outstretched arm, the custom until April 1943 when it was banned because it looked like a Nazi salute. Photos were for a Life Magazine feature, but were not printed during the war because of anti Japanese feelings.

PG. 45 "In fact, both…" First Lady, Eleanor Roosevelt, one of Stanley's heroes, was one of the first to speak out about this and enlisted the help of her friend, Clarence Pickett, leader of the American Friends, to get college-aged students back to college. By Order of the President, Greg Robinson, Harvard University Press (Cambridge, MA, 2001)

PG. 48 "Jan. 14, 1943…" The use of asterisks in this entry indicate two instances where I have edited language that was commonly acceptable when written in 1943, but are now considered offensive and whose use today would reverse

Stan's meaning. The word in brackets was substituted to convey meaning. The original words can be found online at www.JANM.org. These are the only edits in the diary.

PG. 48 "In many ways…" Stan's hero, George Washington Carver, the great African American scientist and inventor who discovered different uses of the peanut plant and sweet potato, was an early environmentalist and promoter of sustainable agriculture, and a tireless advocate and example of the equal abilities of the races.

PG. 49 "Long before the…" National Forensic League's topic for 1942-43 was Resolved: That a federal world government should be established. A Federal World Government After the War, *Scholastic Magazine*, Vol. 41, no. 12, Dec. 7-12, 1942. 14-15.

PG. 49 "Vice President Henry…" Wallace's World Organization speech, given on the anniversary of Woodrow Wilson's birth calls for the United Nations to take up the torch of the League of Nations, the organization that the United States had not supported after WWI. In his Common Man essay he writes, "India, China, and Latin America have a tremendous stake in the people's century. As their masses learn to read and write, and as they become productive mechanics, their standard of living will double and treble." Years later Wallace, in his bid to become President of the United States, he refused to speak to segregated audiences. His key speeches are on http://newdeal.feri.org/wallace/links.htm.

PG. 55 "To add insult…" For fuller explanation of the so-called loyalty questionnaire, *American Inquisition*, Eric Muller, University of North Carolina (Chapel Hill, 2007)35-38.

PG. 57 "Yesterday I went…" Not everyone accepted incarceration. Lincoln Kanai, Sec., San Francisco YMCA, wrote to DeWitt 3/6/42 asking for a hearing board for aliens and citizens and consideration for those with sons in the armed forces. He also asked for custodianship of property so evacuees would not lose capital assets. There was a freeze on travel outside the evacuation area, but Kanai went to a YMCA conference in Wisconsin. He was arrested and sentenced to prison. Personal Justice Denied, 115, CWRIC

PG. 58 "An editorial in…" HMS, Feb. 6, 1943
PG. 58 "While Stan seems…" Reports of students debates in the classroom are in Interviews with Teachers, Community Analysis, Sept 1,1943.;WRA RG 210, Reel 16, NARA.

PG. 60 "The government's volunteer…" The 805 figure comes from Resistance: Challenging America's Wartime Internment of Japanese Americans, pg. 101, William Minoru Hohri, et al. (Epistolarian, Lomita. CA, 2001) There were some Hawaiian Nikkei who were incarcerated and brought to the mainland, but they were the exception. There were too many Hawaiian Nikkei and they were needed in vital jobs supporting the war.

PG. 62 "Eventually close to…" Segregation was not complete. Some who signed "yes-yes" and were loyal chose to remain at Tule Lake rather than move yet again. Many young people who would have signed "yes-yes" were forced to go with their families who wished to return to Japan.

PG. 65 "By early March…" Robertson's threatening memo was excerpted in HMS, March 6, 1943.

PG. 67 "To Dillon Myer…" Guy Robertson letter to Dillon Myer, JERS, M1.10, BANC.

PG. 71 "In spite of…" By spring, 1943 H.M. had a new high school with a huge gym. Even before it officially opened kids sneaked in to toss basketballs and thrill to the vast space. It held 700 people for games and 1,000 for performances. Teams from Wyoming and Montana came to play the Heart Mountain Eagles.

PG. 71 "Woke up at…" The majority of Heart Mountaineers were Buddhists, but there were a great number of Christian churches and many conversions took place in the camps.

PG. 72 "It seems that…" Three men were given mock trials and were put to death. Five other men were kept as prisoners on a starvation diet. Their health was destroyed. One of the five died.

PG. 73 "Lt. Col. Jimmy…" B-25s were land-based planes and had never before taken off from a ship at sea. Unlike the Japanese torpedo bombers used on Dec. 7th, these were large and complex bombers doing something they weren't designed for.

PG. 73 "A cartoon in…" *Denver Post* April 22, 1943, 1.

How Come?

The cartoonist used the same format to attack the Nikkei on so-called "coddling," claiming that they were eating better inside the camps than civilians on the outside. It was a total lie.

PG. 73 "In a speech…" Denver Post, April 25, 1943, 2.

PG. 74 "At Camp Shelby…" Press release Office of War Information, April 23, 1943, WRA Records, Bancroft.

PG. 86 "16 days have…" Munda was a Japanese air base in the Solomon Islands that fell after six long weeks of fighting.

PG. 92 "One of those…" After the war Frank returned to New York and married Martha. He wrote to her all through the war and she saved his letters. Sadly, when he found the letters years later he insisted on destroying them all.

1944 (PG. 96–122)

PG. 100 "We the members…" Fair Play Committee Bulletin of Mach 1944. Excerpt from A Matter of Conscience, ed. Mike Mackey (Powell: Western History Publications, 2002) 55,

PG. 100 "Their trial was…" In 1947 the resisters were pardoned by President Harry S. Truman.

PG. 112 "Valedictory Speech…" HMS May 12, 1944

PG. 118 "Although Stan tells…" Letters to and from O. Leon Anderson were found in Stan's WRA Evacuee File, National Archives, Washington, D.C.

Stan was in awe of his friend Paul Mayekawa, valedictorian 1944.

PG. 122 "Stan reported for…"

These send-offs became a sad and constant ritual as the community turned out to say good-bye to more and more Nisei sons who were drafted into the 442nd.

Beyond the Diary (PG. 123–141)

PG. 135 "In time, the…." The emblem of the 442nd RCT was an arm holding up a torch. It was originally designed with a yellow arm that was rejected as offensive and redone in red, white, and blue.

442nd Insignia

PG. 136 "Today for the…" St. Augustine was actually founded in 1565.

PG. 137 "Everything was not…" Frank's name is listed as a visiting GI in the HMS, Nov. 25, 1944. The same paper carries a story about the death of Ted Fujioka, the first student body president of Heart Mountain High school. Bad news of the growing number of dead and dying at the front continued to arrive daily to the Nikkei community.

PG. 139 "Among the soldiers…" When a soldier was killed, the deep blue star was covered with gold. Some families had as many as five or more blue stars, but many were lucky enough not to have any gold stars.

1945 (PG. 142–182)

PG. 144 "Tad insists that…" Many soldiers not only did basic training, some were sent on to gunnery school or other specialties. That would have lengthened their training time. Tad was drafted in the spring, the war in Europe ended; the 442nd's need for replacements was not as urgent as in January 1945.

PG. 145 "For six days…" After the rescue, according to legend, when Gen. Dahlquist ordered the 442nd to assemble for a ceremony he reprimanded a Nisei officer for failing to assemble the entire regiment. The officer is said to have answered, "General, this is the regiment. The rest are either dead or in the hospital."

PG. 146 "Stanley's next letter…" Stanley signed his Sept 24th letter with Japanese symbols ??? that mean Kunio. This is the only letter he signs in Romaji as Kunio.

PG. 144 "But the overriding…" Inouye's quote of his father's words to him, as told in *Beyond Glory, Medal of Honor Heroes in their Own Words,* Larry Smith (New York: Norton, 2006), 40.

PG. 145 "For six days…" Lost Battalion stories often make it sound like the men were all Texans. In fact, only a fraction of them were from Texas. Their nickname came from the 36th Division's origins with the Texas National Guard. Walter Okitsu, of Go For Broke Education Center, pointed out that history books often mistakenly portray the 36th Division as Southern racists who needed rescuing. But the men of the 36th had been in tough battles in Italy, and went on to fight in France and Germany after the 442nd left.

PG. 145 "In June of…" The 100th Infantry Battalion was known as the "Purple Heart Battalion" because of their horrific losses. The Purple Heart is awarded to soldiers killed or wounded in battle. Information on battle from The Rescue of the Lost Battalion, Go For Broke National Education Center.

PG. 145 "Long after these…" After the war, in a ceremony, Gen. Dahlquist tried to shake the hand of Lt. Col Singles, suggesting that they let bygones be bygones. Singles saluted Dahlquist, but refused to shake his hand for carelessly spilling the blood of thousands of Nisei soldiers. Homeofheroes.com.

PG. 145 "In the face…" The army needed not just more Japanese Americans for the 442nd, they assigned segregated African American troops to leave the supply lines and take up combat roles they had previously been denied.

PG. 145 "Stanley and 1,214…" Champagne Campaign. Go For Broke Education Center.

PG. 147 "Stan's $60 a…" Modern military pay scale http://www.dfas.mil/militarypay.html

PG. 147 "More than a…"We do not have the letters that Stan wrote to his sister Sach, but we know he saw her in New York City before he left for Europe. In fact, they went to see the Broadway musical Oklahoma!

PG. 153 "For a person…" Paris was held by the Germans for four years until the Allies liberated the city on August 25, 1944. Stanley got there six months later, but not for long.

PG. 153 "After days on…"Champagne Campaign, Journal of Battle Campaigns, Echoes of Silence, DVD.

PG. 158 "Their objective was…" German soldiers knew they were outnumbered and could not match the artillery, manpower, and airpower of the Allies. Many wanted to retreat or surrender but Hitler ordered them to fight to the death or else. German soldiers caught fleeing were immediately shot or hanged as traitors by their own men. Field Marshall Kesserling directed the construction of the fortifications for nine months.

Nisei soldiers of the 100th/442ndRCT capturing surrendering German soldiers in Italy.

PG. 154 "Mama, you still…" Stan's mother took classes in English, floral design, and embroidery. Stan's father played *Sho-gi,* a chess game that has been played for centuries in Japan.

PG. 154 "Stanley and the…" Go For Broke National Education Center.

PG. 155 "From his description…" The Distinguished Service Cross, D.S.C., is the 2nd highest medal of the U.S. Army and some were later upgraded to the Medal of Honor. The Croix de Guerre is a French medal that could be bestowed to an individual or as a unit award for heroic deeds. Takemoto was the only non-officer of the 100th/442nd that received the medal individually. Platoons are usually led by lieutenants, but because of the number of men killed or wounded, platoons of the 100th/442nd were often led by sergeants.

PG. 159 "On one LST…" Champagne Campaign, Journal of Battle Campaigns, Echoes of Silence, DVD.

PG. 160 "They were given…" Champagne Campaign, Journal of Battle Campaigns, Echoes of Silence, DVD 22 March 1945. Arrive at Port in Marseilles. LST's; remained in harbor overnight.

PG. 164 "This was one…" Their motto, "Go for Broke!" came from an expression shouted in dice games when a player would bet everything and 'go for broke!' In battle, that is what these young men did, they gave it everything they had! You can hear firsthand accounts from veterans of the 100th/442nd at www.goforbroke.org.

PG. 166 I interviewed Ray Nosaka when he was

89 at the clubhouse of the 100th Battalion in Honolulu. He told me about an ugly episode that took place in Mississippi when he and 24 other soldiers were taken to a place called Cat Island where they were forced to conduct an idiotic experiment that someone in Washington had dreamed up, an idea born of racist thinking. The experiment was designed to train attack dogs, to kill Japanese soldiers, on the theory that all people of Japanese origin must smell alike. The plan was to train attack dogs using soldiers of the 100th as training bait. Of course the experiment failed. As Ray put it, "Well, they found out that you and I—we smell the same."

Buffalo soldiers on the march into battle.

PG. 167 "The 442nd was…" Many African American soldiers received the Medal of Honor during the Civil War, Indians Wars, and Spanish American War. However, as Jim Crow laws and racial bigotry increased, the paperwork awarding the highest medals for bravery tended to go "lost" or dishonorably withheld. It took until 1997 for 7 veterans to become the only African Americans awarded the Medal of Honor for their heroism during World War II. Only one, former 2nd Lt. Vernon Baker, who fought in the Gothic Campaign, was still alive to receive his award.

PG. 169 "The 442nd had…" The K ration was an emergency meal used in combat because it was light and easy to pack. Each box contained two dried biscuits, cigarettes, toilet paper, gum, sugar, powdered coffee or powdered fruit drink, and such items as "canned meat and egg product." Many soldiers found these meals unidentifiable and barely digestible but were forced to eat them for months on end at times.

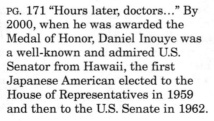

Daniel Inouye as a young officer in 442nd RCT

PG. 171 "Hours later, doctors…" By 2000, when he was awarded the Medal of Honor, Daniel Inouye was a well-known and admired U.S. Senator from Hawaii, the first Japanese American elected to the House of Representatives in 1959 and then to the U.S. Senate in 1962.

He gained nationwide fame with his prominent role in the U.S. Senate's Watergate hearings in 1973-1974.

PG. 172 "On April 23rd, Stan…" Although personnel files were lost in the National Archives fire in St Louis in 1973, we believed Stan was in the 3rd Platoon because Sgt. Tsuneo Takemoto, the sergeant Stan so admired, said in his Goforbroke.org oral history that Daniel Inouye took over "his" unit. Sen. Inouye confirmed this.

PG. 172 "San Terenzo was…" The Bersaglieri were and are elite units of the Italian Army. "Bersaglieri" means "sharpshooters".

PG. 172 "It's unlikely that…" Hitler killed himself on the same day that Stan's V-mail was post marked, April 30th. Hitler was determined not to wait for May 1st, aka May Day, celebrated by the Communists each year nor to end up like Mussolini, killed by Italian partisans.

PG. 173 "For weeks the…" Soldiers of the 100th/442 RCT earned 8,143 individual decorations, among them, 21 Medals of Honor, 33 Distinguished Service Crosses, 559 Silver Star Medals, over 4,000 Bronze Stars, 9,486 Purple Heart Medals, and 8 Presidential Unit Citations. This does not include the medals awarded those in the Military Intelligence Service. Source: Go For Broke

PG. 173 "Company E, 2nd…" There are 2 villages called San Terenzo. The battle was inland, in the mountains of Tuscany, 6 away from the seaside village of San Terenzo. Church story translated, P. Chin. from: "Bersaglieri sulla Linea Gotica" by Davide Del Giudice, (Milano: Ritter Publishing, 2007); "Through heavy German…" Excerpt taken from In Freedom's Cause: A Record of the Men of Hawaii Who Died in the Second World War (1949) with permission from The University of Hawaii Press. National Archives copy from NJAHS-National Japanese Historical Society-San Francisco on the Echoes of Silence DVD

PG. 174 "Before long the…" Bersaglieri sulla Linea Gotica by Davide Del Giudice, (Milano: Ritter, 2007)

PG. 175 "Stanley died in…" Years later a short biography about Stanley says he died on the last day of fighting. In fact, there was sporadic fighting during the next few days. After the 23rd, there were no more active battles against organized units for the 442nd. Unconditional surrender of Axis forces south of the Alps was signed the next day and a ceasefire on the Italian front took place on May 2nd. V-E Day was May 8th. *Po Valley GPO pamphlet, NYPL.*

PG. 180 "The same newspaper..." Roy told his son how a Hawaiian carried him to safety. His story does not preclude the possibility that Stanley went to Roy's aid first and that may be when Stanley was mortally wounded. Memorial service, family on left includes Naochi's brother, Otto, who came to USA with Asano.

PG. 181 "Many years later..." Naoichi had waited 46 years for citizenship. By then, he was a man of 64. Naoichi died in 1972. Asano waited 34 years to become an American. She lived until 1995.

PG. 182 "From the time..." Stanley Hayami's nephew Dan Hayami took this photograph in August 2007 at Evergreen Cemetery in Los Angeles. He discovered that ironically Stan's grave marker says his home state was Wyoming. His mother's brother, James Karatsu, was KIA in France. His grave marker says he was from Colorado. Although he left his family in Amache, a Colorado WRA camp, both of these American GI's were native Californians who died defending their country.

A monument with a statue of Sadao Munemori, first Japanese American to be awarded the Medal of Honor, stands above the gravesites of so many Nisei Sons, young Americans who died defending liberty and the hopes for justice for all.

PHOTO AND DRAWING CREDITS

Great effort has been made to trace and acknowledge owners of copyrighted materials; the publisher would be pleased,however, to add, correct, or revise any such acknowledgment in future printings.

Cover: National Archives (hereafter NARA), Work Permit Card from WRA Evacuee Case File

p. 6: Tempo 1944 Annual (hereafter, Tempo), Bacon Sakatani Collection (hereafter BSC)

p. 7: S.S. Mongolia, collection of Björn Larsson

p. 8: NARA, 90-G-152-2038, Picture brides.

p. 11: Stan's drawing of HM at Night, Stanley Hayami Diary, (hereafter SHD) Japanese American National Museum (hereafter JANM)

p 12: Stanley's photo, NARA, Work Permit Card from WRA Evacuee Case File; Asano and Naochi Hayami, BSC, Frank, Sach & Walt, courtesy Hayami Family.

p. 17: SHD, JANM; Photo, Tempo, BSC

p. 21: Stan's drawing of planes sinking ships, Stanley Hayami Diary (hereafter SHD) Japanese American National Museum (hereafter JANM)

p. 22: Movie and Walking Cold Cartoons, Tempo, BSC

p. 23: Stan's drawing of Pearl Harbor, Frontispiece of Tempo, BSC

p. 24: Stan's drawings, Maybe your dead! SHD, JANM

p. 26: Stan watching UCLA game, SHD, JANM

p 30: Football cartoon, Tempo, BSC

p. 31: Santa, Heart Mountain Reunion Book 2005, BSC

p. 35: Hourglass 1943 SHD, JANM

p. 37: Stan's houses, SHD, JANM

p. 38: Stan's drawing Goh Game, SHD, JANM

p. 39: NARA, 210-G-E591, night school; nightwalker, Tempo, BSC

p. 40: Map of Camp Block, Matthew Weinstein

p. 42: Flag Salute,1943.Photograph by Hansel Mieth, Collection Center for Creative Photography, University of Arizona © 1998 The University of Arizona Foundation

p. 45: NARA, 210-G-E702, Nakadate family; NARA, 210-G-E94, Traditional Dancers

p. 46: Mess Hall, Tempo, BSC

p. 52: NARA, 210-G-E123, swing band

p. 53: NARA, 210-G-E682, skaters

p. 54: Stan's futuristic plane, SHD, JANM

p. 56: Chemistry cartoon, Tempo, BSC

p. 61: Registration, Tempo, BSC

p. 62: Registration, Questionnaire, p4, JANM

p. 63: Stan's Reminiscing, SHD, JANM

p. 64: Eagle Insect and Wiggle My Toes, SDH, JANM

p. 65: "Come and Get it!" SDH, JANM

p. 65: HMS, headline, March 5, 1943

p. 68: Heart Mountain photo, JANM

p. 69: Watch and Lamp, SHD, JANM

p. 70: Stan studying for test, SHD, JANM

TSUNEO

Stan's friend Tsuneo was the boy on the bike on page 74. He was only 15 when he graduated with Stan.